A Collector's Guide to the

Gerber® Baby

® Registered Trademark of Gerber Products Company

The World's Best Known Baby

Featuring Gerber Baby Dolls and Advertising Collectibles

by

Joan Stryker Grubaugh, Ed.D.

The current values for Gerber® Baby dolls are based on the author's purchase price, current price guides and an average of dealers' asking prices. The current values for the Gerber® collectibles were established by a five person panel of antique dealers. Prices vary from dealer to dealer and from one part of the country to another. These established prices should serve only as a guide. They are based on the assumption that the doll or the collectible is in excellent condition. The Author assumes no responsibility for any losses that might occur as a result of consulting this guide.

Additional copies of this book may be ordered from the author @ $39.95. Add $3.00 for Postage.
Inquire about multi copy rates.
Also available from your local antique shop book dealer or distributor.

Please address all correspondence concerning this book to:

Joan Stryker Grubaugh, Ed.D.
2342 Hoaglin Rd. Van Wert, Ohio 45891
Phone (419) 622-4411; Fax (419) 622-3026

Distributed throughout Canada by Collectophile.
3601 Monselet St., Montreal-North, Quebec H1H 2A7
Phone (514) 955-0355; Fax (514) 955-0357

Copyright: Joan Stryker Grubaugh, Ed.D. 1996

Library of Congress Catalog Card Number: 96-94986
ISBN: 0-9654647

Printed by Image Graphics, Paducah, KY

Front cover photo: The beautiful three dimensional presentation of the Gerber Baby head is fashioned in porcelain and measures approximately 11 1/8" x 7 1/2". It was crafted in 1961 for Dan Gerber by Artist / Architect, Ray Jansma, from Fremont, Michigan and remains in the Gerber family. It is mounted on a framed walnut board which measures 15 1/2" x 12". Mr. Jansma is well known for his work in several mediums. In 1953 he designed the beautiful Dan Gerber home on Fremont Lake. Today, he continues to practice his art as well as teaching others in his Fremont studio. **Back cover photo**: 1982 limited edition porcelain doll designed by Neil Estern, crafted by the Shader Doll Co. and produced by Atlanta Novelty, a division of Gerber Products Company. See Plate 123.

Gerber Baby Dolls and Advertising Collectibles
TABLE OF CONTENTS

CONTENTS (CONTINUED)

DEDICATION

This book is dedicated to the memory of a
wonderful mid-Michigan town, and to my family
and friends who helped make it special.

Acknowledgements

Many people have been involved in the writing of this book. The author owes a great deal to everyone who so generously contributed their energy, time and knowledge to help bring about this publication. They have gone far beyond my expectations. I am truly indebted to them, for without their help this book could not have been written.

My foremost thanks goes to Matthew Okkema, retired treasurer and vice-president of Gerber Products Company. Matt was the first person to open doors for me so that I could begin my research by meeting the right people. He saw me through periods of frustration and discouragement by providing me with new avenues to explore and new people to meet. His offer to write a brief history of the Gerber Products Company was gratefully received. Together with his wife, Doris, they made us welcome in their home, as well as providing many of the collectibles pictured in this book.

I am also indebted to several current employees of Gerber Products Company, as well as those who have retired, for their help and encouragement. In particular, I wish to thank the following people.

Van Hindes, Director of Corporate Affairs, for seeing, early on, the possibilities inherent in doing this book and for his encouragement to continue with the project.

Sherrie Harris, Resource Center Manager, who furnished pictures and material from the Corporate archives which have been used extensively throughout this book.

Jane Jeannero, Senior Corporate Attorney, and Cheryl Sloan from the Corporate legal department, for their legal advice and direction.

I also want to acknowledge all those people who allowed their dolls and/or collectibles to be photographed:

Dolls: Ellen Cappadonia and Barbara Maxson from Fremont, MI., Marian Hart, Green Bay, WI, Jill Nihart, Bryan, OH, and Bonnie Shires, Lemington, Ontario, Ca.

Collectibles: Shirley Brooks, Kyle Converse, Gerber Corporate Archives, Barbara Howard, Bob Johnston, Matt and Doris Okkema, Robert Robart, and Lois Witte from Fremont, MI. Marian Hart from Green Bay, WI and Sue Burness, Paulding, OH.

I want to thank Kyle Converse, Kim Duer, Elma De Young, Richard Harris and Bob Robart from Fremont, MI for helping to date and price the collectibles.

A big "thank you" also, to all those people who answered my ads for dolls and collectibles. I was quite amazed to learn the number and variety of dolls that were made. Likely, there are other dolls that I have not as yet identified. Hopefully, they, as well as other collectibles, will surface by the time the book is revised.

A special thank you to Edward Mobley, Medina, OH, for allowing us to visit his beautiful home and for telling us about the involvement of the Sun Rubber and Arrow

Companies with Gerber and the making of the 1955 and 1965 Gerber dolls.

My thanks to Ann Turner Cook for agreeing to write about her life since she was immortalized as the Gerber Baby, an act she acknowledges to be much less important than her role as a wife, mother, teacher and grandmother.

I also want to acknowledge the librarians in Barberton, OH, and Fremont, MI for their help in retrieving information needed for this book. Thank you to Ray and Donna Rumble, Scott, OH for their help with computer searches and Bob and Joan Bauer, Green Bay, WI. for their research on the silver manufacturing companies.

To a good friend and my computer mentor, Bill Farina, who was always ready to "rescue" me from yet another "emergency", I thank him more than I can express. I was a computer illiterate when I started to write. By the end of the book, with Bill's help, I felt I had conquered the impossible!

To all others who have contributed and have not been mentioned by name, I thank you, also.

Lastly, and most importantly, I thank my husband, Beryl, for his patience and understanding through these many months that this book and the computer have absorbed my life. I thank him for his moral support, for proof reading the manuscript and for accompanying me as I traveled about doing my research. It has been a real team effort.

Professional photographers were Paul Burk, Fremont, MI, and Photography by Lynn, Van Wert, OH. Amateur photographers were Dr. Loren Hart, Green Bay, WI, and the author. Photos of many of the Gerber Identity Items were furnished by Group II Communications, Hales Corners, WI. Photos of the Growing Toys Group were furnished by Toy Biz, Inc. New York. A big thank-you to all of you!

Preface

The first Gerber® Baby dolls were manufactured in 1936. These dolls were made of cloth. The manufacturer is unknown. Since that time six different companies working with leading artists, craftsmen, and designers have attempted to capture the charm of the charcoal drawing done by Dorothy Hope Smith of her friend's baby, Ann Turner (Cook). This drawing became known as The Gerber Baby, the trademark of Gerber Products Company which is located in Fremont, Michigan. My research has uncovered over 130 different versions of the Gerber Baby doll.

I bought my first Gerber® Baby doll in 1981 when it was offered to stockholders as a special purchase. It was to be a gift to my first grandson. Several years later I decided to get one for myself. I found I had to get one from an antique dealer and pay $65.00, which was three times more than I had paid in 1981. I knew my sister had been collecting the Gerber dolls, as well as other dolls, for some time. In the past year I have run into people who say they, too, collect Gerber® Baby dolls or Gerber collectibles. When they find out I am from "the home of Gerber Baby Food", the questions begin. This book hopes to answer those questions by presenting one complete, comprehensive source of information about the Gerber Baby dolls and Gerber collectibles. I had no idea what I would find when I started my research. It has been a rewarding experience.

A word about the Dolls in Part 1

Since only one company manufactured the dolls at any one time the section on the baby dolls is organized by: the manufacturer, year, the doll's description, its accessories, the marketing program, and whether it came as a premium. If known, the number of dolls sold is included. The current value is reported sepa-

rately in the section, *Photo Index and Price Guide Part 4*. Except for the porcelain dolls, the life-like Gerber Baby dolls were usually purchased more as a toy gift for a child than as a collector item.Consequently, they are often well worn. Finding the early dolls with their original clothing, accessories, and packaging is difficult, but not impossible. Since original packaging is important to many collectors it should be noted that dolls ordered as premiums, or through direct sales from Gerber Products Company in Fremont, Michigan, came packaged in brown cardboard boxes the size of the doll. Retail purchased dolls came in decorative boxes and often included many more accessories than the direct order dolls.

The name Gerber® and the Baby® head are registered trademarks and can not legally be reproduced without permission. Identifying characteristics of the Baby head are an open/closed, rose bud shaped mouth with a molded tongue, a molded top knot of hair, round eyes which are blue in White dolls and brown in Black dolls. Other dolls may match this description but there is no mistaking a Gerber Baby doll. As will be noted later, dating of the doll's head did not begin until 1965. (Sun Rubber, 1955-1959, did not date the head.) Five companies produced the dolls between 1965-1996. Atlanta Novelty, a Division of Gerber Products Company (1979-1985) and Lucky Ltd., (1989-1992) changed the date on the head to match the birth date of each changing model as did Toy Biz, Inc. (1994-1996). Arrow Industries (1965-1968) used the 1965 date, Amsco Industries, Inc., a Milton Bradley Company (1972-1973) used 1972.

A word about the Collectibles in Parts 2 & 3.

Collectibles, other than dolls, were made

using the Gerber Baby trademark adjusting it to fit the size of the item. The Gerber Baby became the "World's Best Known Baby", and remains so today. Most promotional items had both the name Gerber and the Baby head printed on them. However, some had either one or the other.

Gerber began to issue premium items in the 1930's, but discontinued them during World War ll (1941-1945), and began again in 1946. In the 70's Gerber began to expand their interest beyond baby food into merchandising of baby care items and life insurance.

During the 80's Gerber initiated a sales program of promotional items which were available to employees, stockholders, and retirees. The 90's have seen a greater emphasis on mass merchandising and entering into the area of toys that grow with your child. However, the sale of high quality food for infants and toddlers remains their first priority.

Besides premiums and sale items Gerber made available many "freebie" souvenirs through its company tours, the Tourist Center, and special events which they sponsored.

An especially exciting area to collect is the early employee related paraphernalia ranging from tools and work related items to clothing. In 1949 Mrs. Dan Gerber (Dorothy) began her advice column "Bringing Up Baby", with helpful hints she had collected as a mother of 5. The column appeared in Gerber Products Company ads in all the leading household and women's magazines as well as in medical journals. The column continued through 1968. From 1943 until 1948 Mrs. Gerber's column was titled "One Mother to Another". Advise articles began to appear in the ads as early as 1940 to which Mrs. Gerber signed her name. Dan Gerber also spoke to parents through the ads in 1958 and 1959. His picture was often in the ad. Mr. Gerber was very protective of his family and seldom did the children or grandchildren appear in the ads. However, I have found three which I have included in the magazine ad section at the end of the book.

The first Gerber Baby Food ads appeared in the November, 1928, issues of *Good Housekeeping Magazine*, *Child Life*, and *Junior Home*, and in the December issue of *Children*, later to be called *Parents Magazine*. November, 1928 saw ads in the *Journal of the American Medical Association* and the *Michigan Tradesman*. Advertising through magazines and cents off coupons in the stores were important parts of the promotional efforts of the company from the beginning.

Photos of the dolls and collectibles in the author's collection have been used throughout. Credits are given for "guest" dolls and / or collectibles used to supplement the collection. When known, a brief history of each doll manufacturing company is given and collectibles are dated.

A short history of the development of Gerber Products Company, written by Matthew Okkema, a retired Vice President of the company, suppliments the author's article titled, "The Development Of An Idea. A personal account of her life as the Gerber Baby, written by Ann Turner Cook, adds a great deal of interest to the book. In his article about the differences in making toys of rubber or vinyl, Edward Mobley uses his years of experience as a designer for Sun Rubber Company and later having his own line of vinyl toys produced by Arrow Moulded Products Company. Sections on Gerber doll Look-A-likes, an index, a bibliography, and the author's biography conclude the book. A Photo Index and Price Guide is included.

*The first ads for Gerber baby foods were in 1928.
They appeared in many household magazines.*

Photo courtesy of Gerber Products Company Corporate Archives.

THE DEVELOPMENT OF AN IDEA

What started out to be nothing more than a favor for his wife, turned into the world's leading baby food and infant care company. In 1927 Dan and Dorothy Gerber were the proud parents of two small daughters. The family pediatrician believed that infants should be started on solid foods by the time they were five months old. Until that time only Clapp was making prescription baby food, available in drug stores. One summer Sunday at suppertime, Mrs. Gerber was straining peas for baby Sally, while her husband, Dan, waited anxiously for her to finish. They were running a little late for an evening's engagement. Mrs. Gerber gave her husband the food and strainer and asked him to see if he could do it any faster. From that experience he realized what a chore it was. Mrs. Gerber questioned why the baby's food couldn't be strained at the family's cannery with the machines that were used to puree tomatoes. She was referring to the Fremont Canning Company, an adult food packer started in 1901. (1)

(1)

(2)

Dan and his father, Frank, agreed to try out Dorothy's idea, and production people spent many months developing strained foods for babies. Sally became the first tester, and babies of friends and employees came next. After receiving many local compliments, groups of pediatricians, nutritionists, grocers, farmers and most importantly, mothers were consulted for insights and ideas. And as they say, "The rest is history".

The Gerber Baby Story:

Through the years the progress and success of Gerber baby foods developed mostly from ingenious marketing strategies, originated by Dan Gerber himself, and then supplemented and carried on by others. In the first year, 1928, Gerber initiated a contest to produce a logo which would represent their new products. In response, Dorothy Hope Smith submitted an unfinished charcoal sketch of her neighbor's baby, Ann Turner (Cook) (2). She told Gerber she would fin-

11

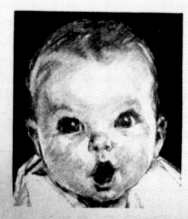

Vegetables for baby

Specially Prepared Strained and Ready-to-Serve

OF vital importance to mothers of young children are these new strained vegetable products. With *absolute safety* they meet the daily problem of baby's vegetable feedings. And they save the many, many tedious hours spent in cleaning, cooking and straining vegetables for baby. With Gerber's Strained Vegetable Products the wholesome vegetable supplement to the milk diet becomes as accurate and simple as A-B-C.

Approved by Leading Authorities

Steam pressure cooked and sealed—sterilized at high temperature—Gerber's Strained Vegetable Products retain most of the valuable mineral salts and vitamin elements lost when vegetables are cooked at home in open vessels. Particularly they conserve the important Vitamin 'C' in which milk is so deficient. All have been tested and approved by Good Housekeeping's Bureau of Foods, Sanitation and Health; the Institutes of The Delineator, Modern Priscilla, Child Life and Junior Home; and leading pediatric authorities. Gerber's Strained Vegetable Soup is based on a famous professional formula.

A Balanced Diet Rich In Vitamins

Gerber's Products are conveniently and economically packed for two full size feedings. Vegetable Soup—Strained Spinach—Carrots—Peas—and Prunes afford the variety required for a balanced vegetable feeding schedule—rich in tooth, bone and body building vitamins. With the normal baby, feedings should begin at from 6 to 8 months. Consult your Doctor for the best feeding schedule for the individual problem of your own baby.

Special Introductory Offer

You must try Gerber's Products yourself to appreciate how good and how convenient they are. The entire Gerber line will be available at leading grocers—25¢ for the 10¼ Ounce can of Soup—15¢ for the 4½ Ounce can of Strained Vegetables. If your grocer is not yet able to supply you—send us today the attached special offer coupon. For your grocer's name and $1.00, we will send postpaid our introductory package containing 2 cans of Soup—and 1 can each of Strained Spinach, Carrots, Prunes, and Peas—enough for a week's supply. Clip and mail the coupon today!

Gerber's *
STRAINED VEGETABLES

Free samples gladly sent on request to physicians or hospitals.

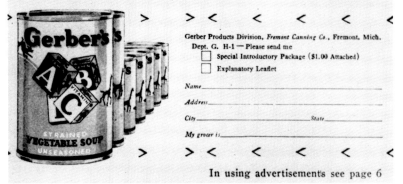

Gerber Products Division, *Fremont Canning Co.*, Fremont, Mich.
Dept. G. H-1 — Please send me
☐ Special Introductory Package ($1.00 Attached)
☐ Explanatory Leaflet

*Name*_____
*Address*_____
*City*_____ *State*_____
*My grocer is*_____

In using advertisements see page 6

(4)

12

ish it if they agreed that this was the size and age of a baby they had in mind. Artist Smith never had a chance to finish it as the Company accepted it just the way it was. (Today, that original drawing is preserved under glass in the Company archives).

Without a doubt the consistent and wholesome use of this charming baby face known as the Gerber Baby has made it a symbol of quality and trust to parents worldwide. Careful advertising, including the long running "Bringing Up Baby" columns, (3) endeared millions of Moms to the company's products. Numerous letters continually came in proudly proclaiming "my baby looks just like the Gerber Baby", and much speculation arose through the years over who actually was the Gerber Baby in the logo. The original Gerber Baby symbol has endured through all the changes that have taken place within the Company. It never has been felt that there was a need to modernize the symbol as many other companies have done to their trademarks. A baby in 1928 looks the same as a baby in any year.

Bringing Up Baby

HINTS COLLECTED BY

Mrs Dan Gerber

(MOTHER OF 5)

Bad Weather Tip. If you're caught short of drying space in an emergency, tip baby's play pen over on its side and use it as an extra drying rack.

Mrs. Gerber

(3)

Marketing:

Right from the beginning Gerber set its sights on the national market. (4) A *Good*

Housekeeping ad in November, 1928, asked women to "Send a dollar and a slip with the name of your grocer and we'll send you six assorted cans of baby food". As the responses poured in salesmen followed up the store leads in cars with horns that played "Rock-a-Bye Baby". (5) This marketing strategy, and others that followed, paid off handsomely. Five hundred ninety thousand (590,000) cans were sold the the first year. One million cans a week were sold in 1941. By 1948, the post-war baby boom demanded two million cans a day!

The primary method for reaching new mothers was always by direct mail. Personalized letters were sent about six weeks after birth, often with cereal samples enclosed, and again at about three months old with strained food coupons. Attractive kits of food, (6) or just the famous Gerber spoon, (7) were also offered as premium items at low prices.

Helpful and image building ads have always appeared in magazines and later in newspapers. (See magazine ad section) In 1948 a new slogan was adopted: *"Babies are our business...our only business"*. Support advertising was sometimes used on radio and television with popular personalities such as Kate Smith, Bud Collier, Captain Kangaroo (8) and Miss Francis in Canada. Tours at all manufacturing plants were very popular until 1990 (9) when replaced by a Visitor's Center, (now closed) at the Fremont, Michigan headquarters. Visitors at the Center were able to see some of the dolls and other premium items from the past, view a 3D movie depicting the world through a toddler's eyes, receive free souvenirs and purchase items from the gift shop. Today these items are all considered very collectible.

(5)

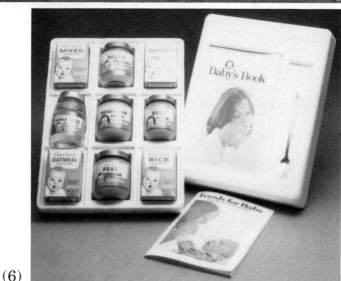

(6)

For handsome International Silver plated baby spoon, send 10¢ plus 6 labels or box tops from Gerber's Baby Foods. Print your name and address carefully. Gerber's, Dept. 12, Fremont, Mich.

Gerber's
Baby Foods

"From a few weeks to a few years"

(7)

(8)

13

Merger:

In 1994, a merger was arranged with Sandoz Ltd., a large Swiss pharmaceutical company, and all of the publicly held Gerber stock was bought up at a premium price. Then, in 1996 Sandoz merged with Ciba Geigy AG, another Swiss drug giant. So now, Gerber Products Company, once a proud independent company owned by the stockholders, is a subsidiary of a Swiss conglomerate. This is a sign of the times, I guess. Will other changes come along as a result of this merger? Meanwhile, production continues, and the Gerber Baby still appears on the baby food and baby care products. However, the Visitor Center is now closed. Gone is the museum. No longer can one view the dolls and pick out souvenirs to remind them of their trip to Fremont to 'see' the Gerber Baby. Another era has come to an end. ...Another adventure has begun. (10)

(9)

(10)

The old company photos were made available through the courtesy of Gerber Products Company Archives. Sherrie Harris, Corporate Librarian.

INTRODUCING THE FIRST GERBER BABY - A REAL LIVING DOLL

Becoming the model for the Gerber Products trademark when I was four months old took no skill on my part. I simply raised my head, opened my mouth, and looked at my mother while she took the photograph that became the principal source for a drawing by an exceptionally talented artist, Dorothy Hope Smith— whose married name was Mrs. Perry Barlow— was a friend of my parents and one who specialized in studies of

children. When she decided to sketch my portrait in 1927, she also referred for the likeness to home film and other photographs.

The following year Gerber Company president Dan Gerber and his wife had a brilliant idea. They converted their vegetable canning business in Fremont, Michigan, into one that made the first canned baby food. When the company sent word to commercial art agencies that they were in the market for a trademark, Mrs. Barlow's agent contacted her, and she sent her large sketch of me. It became the unanimous choice. Although Mrs. Barlow had considered the drawing preliminary, the company wanted it just as it was — and is.

I have always known that I was the model, but the fact made very little difference in my daily life. As I grew up and earned a degree in English at Southern Methodist University in Dallas, people were more impressed by the fact that my father, Leslie Turner, wrote and drew the popular comic strip *Wash Tubbs and Captain Easy*, which was syndicated in more than five hundred national newspapers and several abroad.

It was not until 1950 that I had contact with the Gerber Company. At that time Mrs. Barlow wrote to let me know that another parent had come forward to claim their child was the original Gerber Baby, and she had been called by the company to verify that I was indeed the model. Our artist friend thought that I should have a legal understanding with the company.

In 1951 the Gerber Company clarified the situation by paying me for the right to use my picture. That five thousand dollars came at a fortunate time. My husband, James E. Cook, a criminologist and navy veteran of World War II, had just graduated from the University of Illinois on the G.I. Bill. With the money we were able to buy our first car and make a down payment on a modest little house, at that time in Danville, Illinois.

We had four children while still living in Illinois — the oldest Jan, now a free lance writer in Alexandria, Virginia; Carol, a children's librarian in Silver Springs, Maryland; and twins, Clifford, a stockbroker in St. Petersburg, Florida; and Kathleen, a business executive in Tampa.

In 1959 our family moved to Florida to be near my parents, who lived in Orlando. In a few years I began a career as an English teacher and returned to college, where I received my Master's in English Education at the University of South Florida.

Reporters always eventually heard about the Gerber connection and a story would appear in the local newspapers. Although most people were increasingly interested in the fact that I was a model, in the beginning it became a handicap to me as a teacher. Being America's most famous baby did not enhance my image of authority and junior high students were unmerciful in their teasing. Therefore, I tried hard for several years to keep the news from other students. Finally, after I felt secure at Hillsborough Senior High School in Tampa — where I was to spend twenty-three years — I allowed the school newspaper to run a story and these more mature students were able to process the fact without its affecting the classroom discipline.

In 1978, and in the following years, I began making occasional television appearances on such shows as *Mike Douglas* and *Good Morning America*. My students enjoyed these, and on at least one occasion other teachers allowed their classes to watch a daytime interview and glory in the mention of their school. That same year the Gerber Company flew me to Fremont for a banquet and appearance in the company offices to commemorate the fiftieth anniversary. In 1981 Atlanta Novelty Company sent me a collection of Gerber baby dolls, including a beautiful limited-edition porcelain doll.

I served the last fifteen years of my twenty-six year teaching career as English Department Head at Hillsborough High. I have always considered my contribution as a teacher much more significant than the fact that a gifted artist was able to make me an internationally recognized symbol for babies. In the meantime our children increased our good fortune by presenting us with ten intelligent, problem-free grandchildren.

In 1989 I retired to devote more time to a lifelong ambition to write. In this I have had some success, having published a short story, several articles, and in 1995 placed two mystery novel manuscripts with a literary agent in New York. Perhaps the Gerber Baby relationship had a subconscious influence. A baby is integral to the plot of the first, a toddler to the second.

In 1990 my husband retired from his position as a Major in the Hillsborough County Sheriff's Office, and now we frequently indulge in a hobby of pontoon boating on Florida's rivers, where I find many of my ideas for settings and stories. In 1997 we will celebrate our fiftieth wedding anniversary. Perhaps completing fifty years of a strong marriage, and rearing four fine citizens who all have their own stable families, is a more important achievement than either of our past careers, our current interests, or my identity as the Gerber Baby.

Ann Turner Cook

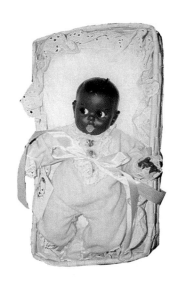

PART 1
GERBER® BABY DOLLS

"LET'S QUIT, MOTHER ...WE CAN'T BEAT GERBER'S VEGETABLE SOUP!

"In spite of all the work it takes to get a lot of different vegetables together, clean them, strain them, (and have a lot of them left over), you can't improve on the wonderful soup that comes out of those pretty blue and white Gerber cans.

"You see, mother, those Gerber vegetables are *Home Grown,* an hour or less by truck from the Gerber kitchens. No chance for them to lose their food values from travelling or storage. And when they are strained and cooked, no air touches them to destroy any of their vitamins, and there is no pouring off mineral salts in cooking water, either.

And this is important, too, Mother
"As vegetable soup is one of the first of my more solid foods, the Gerber people have made a careful study to find out just what should

be put into it. They say it's a 'well-balanced nutritive combination of strained carrots, peas, spinach, rice, barley, beef, tomatoes and celery'. What I say is that it is a grand meal.

"Will you please ask doctor when we may start on Gerber's?"

Only Gerber's Offer All These Advantages

Pedigreed Seeds—developed by expert horticulturists for prize vegetables of highest nutriment.

Controlled Farms—for proper soil, and harvesting at full ripeness.

Home Grown—within an hour from our kitchens to prevent appreciable loss of quality.

Shaker-Cooked—after scientific straining at correct temperatures with air excluded for mineral and vitamin protection in high degree. Each sealed can is mechanically shaken for even cooking throughout.

Gerber's Strained Cereal made from selected whole grains; Gerber's Prunes are from the Santa Clara Valley of California, which also raises Gerber's Apricots. Apples used are Michigan Grimes Golden.

Gerber's
Shaker-Cooked Strained Foods
STRAINED VEGETABLE SOUP—TOMATOES—GREEN BEANS
—BEETS—CARROTS—PEAS—SPINACH—PRUNES—CEREAL—
APRICOT AND APPLE SAUCE—LIVER SOUP

You are Invited to Visit our Plant when Touring in Michigan.

A Delightful Gift For Your Baby
A fine stuffed doll of good quality sateen, boy doll in blue, girl doll in pink. Sent for 10c and 3 Gerber labels.
GERBER PRODUCTS COMPANY, FREMONT, MICHIGAN   46
(In Canada, Gerber's are *grown and packed by* Fine Foods of Canada, Ltd., Tecumseh, Ontario.)

Name_____

Address_____

City_____ State_____

Actual size, 8 in. high

Check items desired:
☐ Boy Doll   ☐ Girl Doll   ☐ Mealtime Psychology, a free booklet on infant feeding.
☐ Baby's Book, on general infant care, 10c additional.

GERBER® BABY DOLLS
1936 -1939

MANUFACTURER
UNKNOWN

8 INCH GIRL, SILK SCREENED
SATEEN CLOTH—**PREMIUM**

8 INCH BOY, SILK SCREENED
SATEEN CLOTH—**PREMIUM**

Plate 1

The **first Gerber® baby dolls** were cloth dolls made of silk-screen sateen. They measured **8 inches long, 2 3/4 inches wide at the top, 5 3/4 inches wide at the bottom, and 1/2 inch in depth**. They were filled with cotton type stuffing with heavy overcast stitching around the outside. The dolls were shipped in color coordinated boxes; pink for the girl and blue for the boy. An enclosed folder, *A New Flavor Treat for This Year's Gerber Babies,* extolled the advantages "of the latest in baby food processing-shaker cooking". **

MARKETING: **PREMIUM**: $.10 and 3 Gerber labels. Number sold: 26,690*

* *Gerber Dolls*
  Gerber Products Company
  Corporate Library and Archives
  September 17, 1981

** *Wolfe, A. The First Gerber Dolls*

Plate 1. The Gerber® baby girl doll wears a long pink dress with matching booties, bonnet and sweater with a collar and a sewn-on pink ribbon. She holds a blue stuffed dog in her right hand and a blue and white-labeled can of Gerber baby food in her left. **Plate 2**. Note the continuation of the sweater and skirt pattern in the back view.

Doll from Gerber Products Company Archives.

Plate 2

19

1936-1939

Plate 3. The Gerber® baby boy doll wears a blue pram suit with mittens. He has a stuffed duck in his right hand and a can of Gerber baby food in his left hand. **Plate 4** shows that the pattern of the boy's pram suit continues to the back.

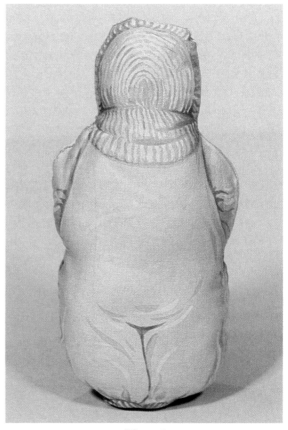

Plate 3   *Plate 4*

Gerber® Baby Dolls
1955-1959 Sun Rubber Company
Second Premium Doll

The first "real" Gerber® baby doll was born in 1955. Sculpted by artist Bernard Lipfert, and manufactured by the Sun Rubber Company, this adorable **12 inch** drink and wet, cry-baby doll was to set the stage for future generations of Gerber baby dolls. Fashioned with a little rose-bud, open/close mouth with a molded tongue and the familiar top knot of hair, the Gerber baby's likeness was captured in the form of a baby doll. The doll's head was made of soft vinyl while its body, arms and legs were of rubber. It had inserted plastic eyes. The head, arms and legs were movable.

Plate 5. The little charmer came dressed in a diaper pinned in front, and a bib inscribed "Gerber Baby". Several accessories were included in the **Premium** offer: a clear glass nurser with plastic nipple and black collar (embossed Sun Babe), four miniature Gerber cereal boxes, a metal bowl colored blue on the outside and white on the inside, and a blue plastic spoon. * The Premium offer was discontinued June 30, 1959.

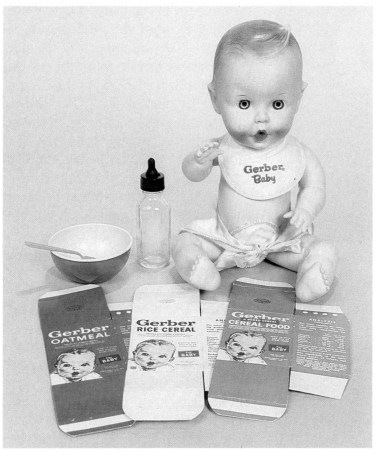

Plate 5

MARKS: Unlike future dolls Sun Rubber Dolls did not carry the date on the neck or body.

Marked on back of neck:
GERBER BABY / ©Gerber Products Co.
Marked above squeaker:
MFG. By / The Sun Rubber Co./Barberton, Ohio USA/Under One or More
U.S.Pat
211862, 2160739, 2552216/ 2629131, 2629134, other Pat. .Pend.

Premium: $2.00 and 12 labels or box tops .

* *Gerber Dolls*
Gerber Products Co.,1981
Accessories courtesy of Gerber Products Company Archives

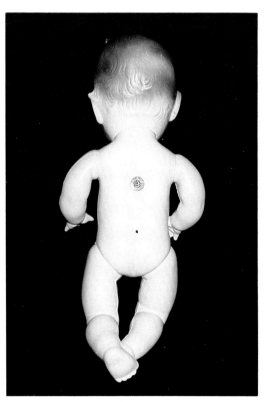

Plate 6

Plate 7

12 Inch Sun Rubber Company First "real" Gerber® Baby Doll

The Sun Rubber Company of Barberton, Ohio was the first company licensed by Gerber Products Company to make a doll that captured the likeness and charm of the famous Gerber® baby face. Designed by artist Bernard Lipfert the 12 inch doll with vinyl head and rubber body continues to be the most wanted Gerber® baby doll. A sure winner from the start the doll was available from 1955-1959 as a **Premium** offer, and in the 12 inch, 13 inch and 18 inch sizes for the retail market. The 18 inch doll had a vinyl body and has held up better than the rubber bodies through the years. All dolls were drink and wet "Mama" dolls. The 12 inch doll had non-movable inserted eyes, while the 13 inch and 18 inch dolls had sleep eyes. All the dolls had movable head, arms and legs.

Although the Sun Rubber Company is credited with making this group of dolls, Arrow Rubber and Plastics Corporation in New Jersey was also involved. During World War ll the Sun Rubber Company discontinued toy making and geared up to produce products needed for the War effort. With its confidence in its future bolstered by its successful war years, the company invested in the latest technology of heavy metal 2 piece molds needed for making rubber toys again. However, plastics and synthetics which used a simpler one piece mold process, began taking over the industry. Manufactures were able to create designs with better detail and obtain better colors with the new vinyls. Also, the one piece molds did not leave mold marks. Arrow Corporation was set up for the new process. Sun Rubber Company contracted with Arrow Corporation to make the 12 inch doll heads and probably the limbs of the 18 inch doll which show no mold marks. Sun Rubber Company used its own 2 piece molds when it produced the vinyl heads of the 13 inch and 18 inch dolls, and the vinyl body of the 18 inch doll. It used rubber in its molds when it made the 12 inch and 13 inch bodies. Seam lines, or mold marks are signs it was made with the Sun Rubber Company molds.*

The two piece mold marks are visible in **Plates 6 and 7**.

The Sun Rubber Company, which began by making wonderful rubber toys in 1923, closed its doors in 1974.*

* Edward Mobley, Former designer for Sun Rubber Company and Arrow Molded Plastics Corporation: Personal Interview, November 27, 1995. (see "Is It Rubber or Vinyl?" p.202)

Gerber® Baby Dolls
1955 Canadian Version
Viceroy / Sunruco Company

A Canadian version of the 12 inch Premium Gerber baby® doll was made by the Viceroy / Sunruco Company of Canada, and offered to the Canadian market for one year. It came dressed in a diaper and bib marked Gerber®, the same as the Sun Rubber doll. It was distributed through media advertising as well as by Miss Francis and the Ding Dong School TV program. The body of the Sunruco doll is the same as the Sun Rubber doll except for the marking on the back which reads :

A Viceroy / Sunruco Doll
Made in Canada / Patent Pending

The molded vinyl head of the Canadian doll is very curly compared to the American version. **Plates 8 and 9** compare the two heads. All Canadian Sunruco dolls had very curly hair. The original Sun Rubber dolls all had the straighter hair. However, since Sun Rubber dolls were made over a period of three years, compared to one year for the Sunruco dolls, an over supply of heads may account for the Sunruco doll's head being found on a Sun Rubber doll's body. The Viceroy /Sunruco dolls are very rare. To find one in good condition is a real fine.

Doll on left, with Sunruco head, from Marian Hart collection.

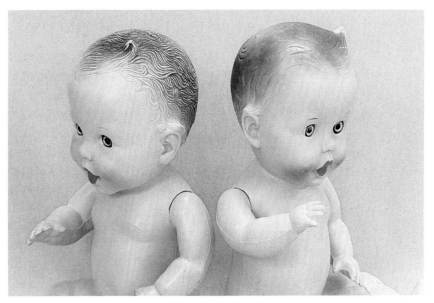

Plate 8

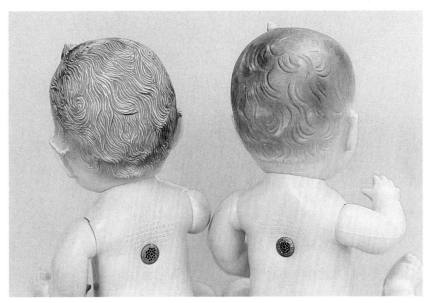

Plate 9

Gerber® Baby Dolls
1955-1958
Sun Rubber Company
12 Inch Retail

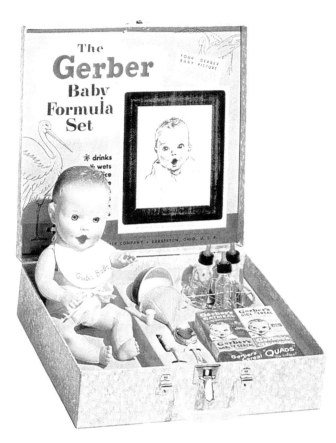

Plate 10

Plate 10. The **Gerber Baby Formula Set** by Sun Rubber Company included a **12 inch** drink and wet "Mama" doll for the retail trade. It came dressed in a diaper and a bib marked GERBER® BABY. Booties were included in the carrying case. Other accessories included a four pack of miniature Gerber cereal boxes, formula bowl, "silver" spoon, three bottles in a bottle rack, funnel and a bottle brush. A picture of the Gerber Baby was included. This doll is extremely hard to find in the original case with the accessories. **Plate 11**. Doll dressed in original playsuit with bib.

Plate 11

Marked on back of neck:
GERBER BABY
(c) Gerber Products Co.

**Marks: Unlike future dolls,
Sun Rubber Dolls were not dated.**

Marked on back of body along with patent number:
MFG. BY
SUN RUBBER CO.
BARBERTON, OHIO USA

MARKETING: Retail Stores:
Appeared in 1955 Sears Roebuck Co. Toy Catalog

The pictures are from the 1955 Sun Rubber Company catalog, courtesy of Edward Mobley.

Gerber® Baby Dolls
1955-1958
Sun Rubber Company
13 inch Retail

Plate 12. The 13 inch Sun Rubber Company drink and wet Gerber® baby doll is identical to the 12 inch doll in shape, but has a vinyl body and sleep eyes. Dressed in a diaper and a bib marked "Gerber", she came in a carrying case. Her accessories included a metal bowl, which was blue on the outside and white on the inside, a silver plated spoon, three bottles in a rack, funnel, a bottle brush, and a weighing scale. A stunning wardrobe was included. The photo is from the 1955 Sun Rubber Co. Catalog. This doll is considered to be very rare with, or with out, its accessories.

Marked on the back of her head:
GERBER BABY
(c) Gerber Products Co.

Marked on back of body
along with patent numbers:
MFG.BY
SUN RUBBER CO.
BARBERTON, OHIO, USA

MARKETING: Retail Stores.
This group of dolls were shown in the 1955 Sears Roebuck Co. Toy Catalog

Plate 13 -The head of the 13 inch doll is in the Sun Rubber Company collection at the library in Barberton, Ohio.

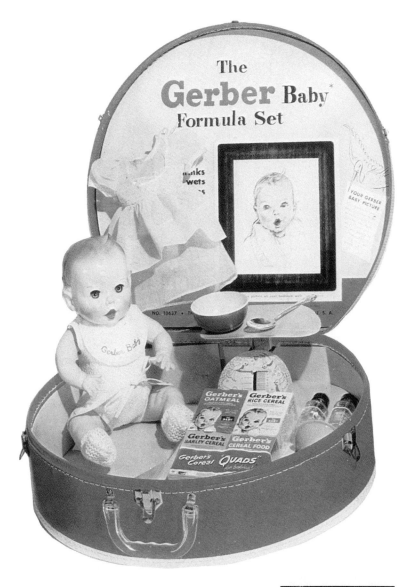

Plate 12

Plate 13

Gerber® Baby Doll
1955-1958
Sun Rubber Company

Plate 14. An **18 inch** Gerber baby doll was ready for the retail market in 1955. Made by Sun Rubber Company she remained the largest of the Gerber baby dolls until Lucky Ltd. made a 21 inch doll in 1990.

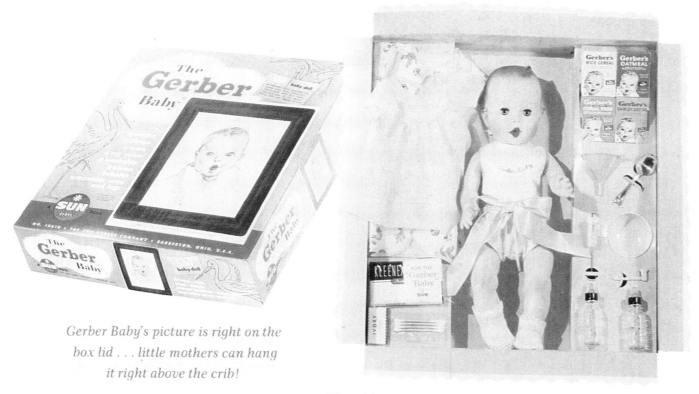

Gerber Baby's picture is right on the box lid . . . little mothers can hang it right above the crib!

Plate 14

Unlike future dolls the Sun Rubber Dolls were not dated.

GERBER BABY
(c)GERBER PRODUCTS CO.

Marked above squeaker on her back:
Mfg. By
THE SUN RUBBER CO.
BARBERTON, OHIO USA

Marked below the squeaker on her back:
Under one or more U.S. Pat.
followed by patent numbers.

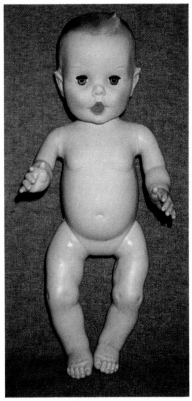

Plate 15

Plate 16

Plate 17

Plate 15. Gone are the bent limbs characterestic of the smaller models. Her life-like glowing complexion with rosy cheeks and a bright rose bud mouth make her a desirable addition to a collection. She has long lashed sleepy eyes that close when she naps. She drinks and wets, cries "Mama", and is able to sit by herself like the other two sizes of dolls. She came with a larger wardrobe than the other two dolls and a few more accessories, but no scale.

Plate 16. Doll in original nightgown.

Plate 17. Doll in original playsuit and bib.

GERBER® BABY DOLLS
1965-1967
MANUFACTURER
ARROW Rubber and Plastic Corp.
14 INCH VINYL- **PREMIUM**

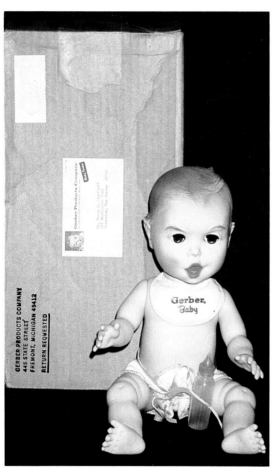

Plate 18

The 1965 doll is the first Gerber baby doll to be dated. Subsequently, all future dolls would be marked with the name GERBER®, along with the date on the back of the neck. The only exception will be the 1983 porcelain dolls which will be covered separately.

Arrow Rubber and Plastic Corporation was a custom molding company which made standard body assemblies for dolls, e.g. arms, legs, and bodies, in 1965. As such, using a company's molds it could quickly and efficiently produce any number of items required. (See Sun Rubber Co. 1955-1959). Through a special licensing agreement with Gerber their designers produced their version of the Gerber® baby doll in 1965.*

This **14 inch** doll has a deep dimple and a lopsided smile which gives a pixie look to the adorable Gerber baby head.

Plate 18.   She came dressed in a diaper and bib marked GERBER® BABY. A plastic nurser with plastic nipple was included in her brown cardboard shipping box. She is the first Gerber baby doll to be inscribed with her "birth"date.

Marked on back of her neck:
Gerber Baby
Gerber Products Co. 1965

* Personal Interview with
Ed Mobley, November 28, 1995.

GERBER® BABY DOLLS
Arrow Rubber and Plastic Corporation
1965-1967

Arrow Rubber and Plastic Corporation was bought by the J.L. Prescott Company in 1968 and changed its name to Arrow Molded Products, a Division of J.L. Prescott Company. They continued to make toys for several companies. One of the companies was Holland Hall who had bought the Gerber Toy Line out of St. Louis. This Gerber Toy Company was originated by an unrelated Gerber family. However, an agreement was reached between the two Gerber companies which allowed the toy company to use the famous Gerber® Baby symbol. Thus, Arrow continued to make toys which bore the name Gerber and the Gerber baby head. My research has not shown that they ever again made a Gerber baby doll. Arrow Company discontinued toy making in 1970 or 1971.*

Plates 19-20. The doll is made of soft vinyl, with sleep eyes. She is a drink and wet doll and cries "Mama".

MARKETING: **PREMIUM**: Described as a $3.98 value the doll sold for 12 Gerber labels or box tops and $2.00. The offer expired June 30, 1967. Number sold: 36,013 **

* Edward Mobley, formerly a designer and sculptor of Disney® toys plus other character toys for the Sun Rubber Company began his own company, The Edward Mobley Company, in 1958. Arrow Rubber and Plastic Corp. was licensed to make the delightful character toys until 1972 when the Arrow Corp. was sold and discontinued making toys. The Edward Mobley Company toys are highly collectible in themselves. (See *"Is It Rubber or Vinyl?"* on page 202)

* Personal Interview, November 28, 1995.

**Gerber Dolls; Gerber Products Co. Corp. Library and Archives, 9/17/81.

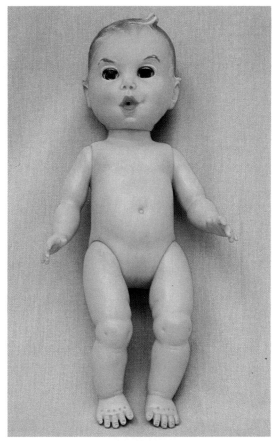

Plate 19

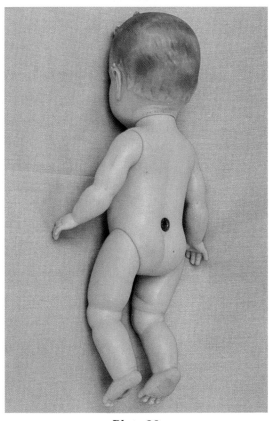

Plate 20

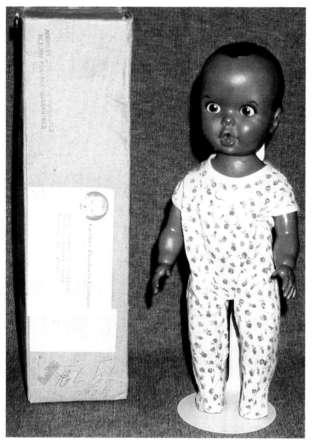

Plate 21

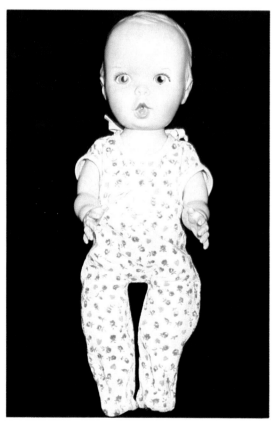

Plate 22

Gerber® Baby Dolls 1972-1973 Amsco Company, A Division of the Milton Bradley Company

Four noticeable changes occurred with the "birth" of the 1972 Gerber® baby dolls. This was the first time that the doll was produced as both a Black or White doll. This was also the first time the White doll was made with yellow molded hair instead of brown. Third, the familiar wispy top knot of hair was much less pronounced, and last, the eyes were painted on instead of being inset eyes or sleep eyes. The Amsco dolls were made in four different sizes. However, the premium dolls were only made in the 10 inch size. White dolls were made in the ten, fourteen, fifteen, and sixteen inch sizes for the retail market. All were marked: The Gerber Baby / Gerber Products Co. / 19©72.

Plates 21 and 22. The **PREMIUM 10 inch** dolls, made of all vinyl, wore a one piece white and pink rose bud sleeper with white binding. The cloth label reads "GERBER® / Made in the British/ Crown Colony of / Hong Kong". She came shipped in a brown cardboard box sized to the doll. **These were the first dolls to be available as Black or White Gerber® baby dolls**.

A contrast between the10 inch premium and retail doll is made in plates **Plates 23 thru 27**.

MARKETING: **PREMIUM**: $2.50 and four labels from any Gerber Toddler Meal, Strained or Junior High Meat Dinner, or two box tops from Gerber Fruit Cereal. Number sold: 60,000*

* *Gerber Dolls*, Gerber Products Co

Gerber Baby Dolls
Amsco
1972-1973

COMPARISON OF HAIR LINES

There are definite differences between the **10 inch retail (left)** and the **10 inch premium dolls (right)** made by Amsco Industries. **Plate 23** compares the hairlines. Notice the dropped down bangs which form a "V" on the forehead of the retail doll. The same hairline is found on all the retail dolls in this group. **Plate 24**. The hair is also much curlier at the neckline on the retail doll than on the premium doll.

Plate 23

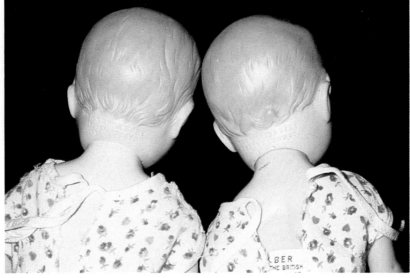

Plate 24

Gerber Baby Dolls
Amsco
1972-1973
COMPARISON OF EYES, FACE, MOUTH, AND FEET

Another noticeable difference is the shape of the mouth which is larger on the retail doll. (right) The eyes are also different as are the feet. Notice the big toe of the premium doll (left) is separate from the other toes. These differences can be seen in **Plate 25** and **Plate 26**.

Plate 25

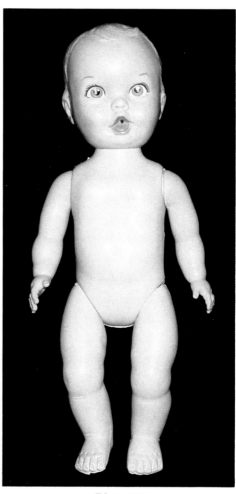

Plate 26

Gerber Baby Dolls
Amsco Dolls 1972
10 Inch Premium and Retail
COMPARISON OF BACK MARKINGS

Plates 27 and **28** compare the backs of the dolls. The retail doll is marked AE which does not appear on the premium doll. A marked impression of dimples in the shoulder blades and a spinal column which can be seen on the premium dolls are not there on the retail dolls.

One difference that can't be shown is the weight of the vinyl. The premium doll as well as the larger retail dolls are made in firm vinyl that would be hard to squeeze. However, the 10 inch retail is made of very light weight vinyl and could be easily crushed. It would appear to the author that these two dolls were designed by different artists.

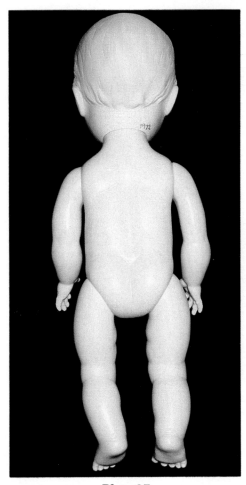

Plate 27

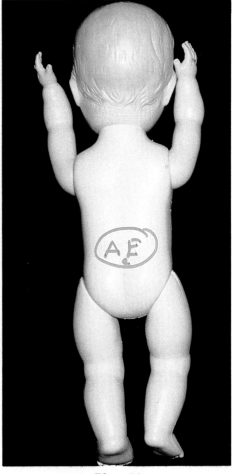

Plate 28

10 Inch Retail Combination
Amsco Dolls 1972-73
Gerber® Baby Dolls

Plate 29. A third doll has been found which is a combination of the 10 inch premium and retail dolls. She has the head and arms of the premium doll but the body and legs of the retail doll. She may have been a special edition doll as the tag on her outfit reads "Gerber/Girl"s World T.M./ A Milton Bradley Co. Warminster, Pa. 18974 / Made in Hong Kong." This is the same name that is on the box for the Amsco 14 inch doll.

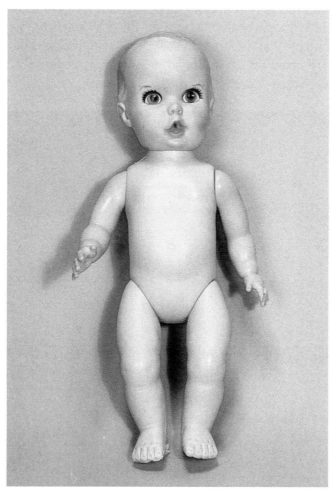

Plate 29

1972 Amsco Retail
Gerber® Baby Dolls

The 10 inch retail dolls have been found in a variety of original outfits.

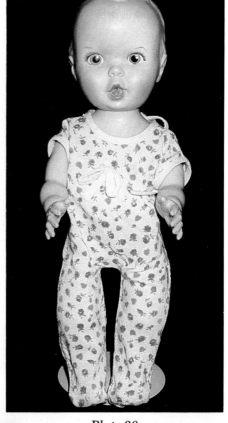

Doll from the
Marian Hart Collection
Plate 32

Plate 31
Doll from the Bonnie
Shires' Collection

Plate 30

Amsco Industries
Gerber® Baby Dolls
1972-1973

Plate 33

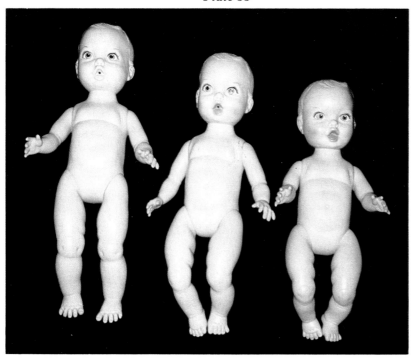

Plate 34

Plate 33. The **14 inch, 16 inch and 18 inch** dolls were made of skin soft vinyl and had a pink cast to their complexions. The feel and thickness of the vinyl is more like the premium doll than like the 10 inch retail doll which feels light and hollow. Their bright blue eyes are painted on and their painted hair is in shades of yellow.

Plate 34 shows that all the bodies exhibit the same navel, folds and creases just like a real baby. Note that the big toe on the right foot of the two smaller sizes is separated and slightly raised from the fourth toe, while all the toes are separated on the 18 inch doll. The bodies are the same length on the two larger dolls but the straighter legs on the 18 inch doll account for the extra inch in overall length. The arms are the same size on the two larger dolls. The 14 inch doll is smaller overall than the other two.

Marked on the back of the neck:
The Gerber Baby
Gerber Products Co.
19(c)72

Amsco Industries
Gerber® Baby Dolls
1972-1973

Plate 35

Plate 36

Plate 35 shows the 14 inch doll dressed in a two piece sun suit. She is packaged with 4 miniature empty Gerber cereal boxes, 4 miniature non-filled jars of Gerber baby food, a plastic bowl and spoon, and a tumbler embossed Gerber® and the Baby face.

Plate 36 shows the 16 inch doll dressed in a 2 piece flowered outfit sitting in her 25" steel framed high chair with a plastic seat, back and tray. This set with its original box is extremely hard to find . . . especially in the condition of the one pictured.

37

Gerber® Baby Dolls
1979 Anniversary
Collector Doll
Atlanta Novelty Company

In 1978 a new Gerber baby doll was introduced to commemorate the 50th Anniversary of the Gerber Products Company. The doll was **17 inches** long with a soft stuffed body and molded vinyl head, arms and legs. The eyes were a 'floating type' and her little rose bud mouth has a molded tongue.

Plates 37 through **42**. The bodies of the Anniversary Dolls were covered in a non-removable suit of either red and white check, blue and white check or yellow and white check trimmed in sewed on white rickrack.

Plate 37

All dolls came with a white eyelet lace trimmed bib and skirt which are removable. They fasten with velcro. The dolls were reissued in 1981, most often without rickrack trim on the checked body suit, and with different clothing items and accessories. All White dolls have light brown hair and blue eyes while the Black dolls have deep brown hair and eyes. All have the floating / flirty eyes that move back and forth often giving them a cross eyed look just like a new born baby. This can be adjusted with a slight movement of the head.

Marked on back of neck:
Gerber Products Co./ © 1979

Marketing: Stockholders and employees were offered the dolls for $18.00. Retail stores sold the dolls for $20.00 to $22.00.

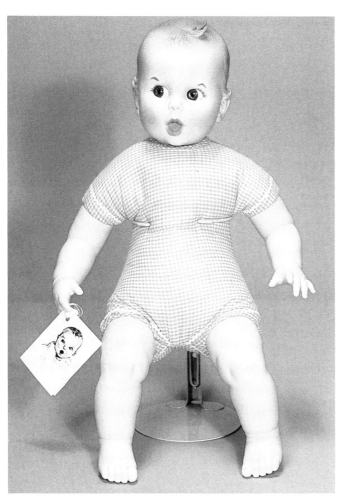

Plate 38

Plate 39

GERBER® BABY DOLLS 1979-1985 MANUFACTURER ATLANTA NOVELTY

Between 1979 and 1985 Atlanta Novelty, a Division of Gerber Products Company , produced a variety of Gerber® baby dolls. "Working from the original charcoal drawing of the Gerber® Baby, Neil Estern, renown artist and sculptor, managed to capture the charm of the drawing"*.

One feature that distinguishes the Atlanta Novelty Gerber® baby doll from other Gerber dolls are the floating, flirty eyes that move back and forth. Although the doll may at

times appear to be cross eyed, a small movement of the head adjusts the eyes back to center. The eyes were purposely made this way to try to copy the way a newborn's eyes often appear. The 1983 "Twins" are the only dolls in this group who do not have these eyes.

Plate 39. The Anniversary doll in red check body suit with eyelet apron and bib.

Plate 40. The red check body suit trimmed in rickrack, This trim is not usually on the reissued dolls.

* Press Releases—-Atlanta Novelty Co./ Gerber Products Co.

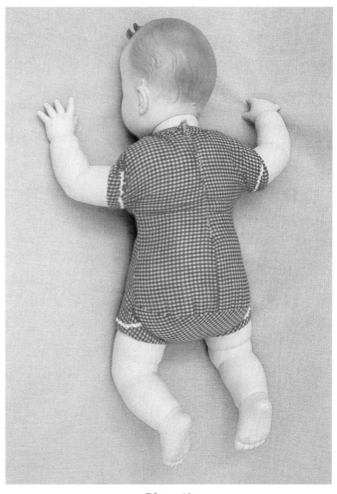

Plate 40

GERBER® BABY DOLLS
1979-1985
MANUFACTURER
ATLANTA NOVELTY

Plate 41

During this period the dolls were produced in several sizes and made of a variety of material combinations. Limited Edition Bisque (Porcelain) dolls, commemorating the 50th anniversary of Gerber Products Company, were made in 1981 (14 inch), 1982 (12 inch), and 1983 (10 inch twins). Crafted by Stephanie and Ken Shader, the bisque arms and legs are dated and the bisque head is also numbered. The bodies are made of soft, stuffed cloth. In 1979 a 17 inch doll, called the Anniversary Doll, was made with a soft body, and vinyl head, arms and legs. This doll was reproduced in 1981 in the same size, and came with different cloths and accessories. Three 12 inch cloth and vinyl dolls were also produced in 1981. **In 1985 both 12 inch and 17 inch dolls were produced in all vinyl. These dolls were the last premium dolls offered by the Company.** The arms and legs were not movable as they were on the other dolls of this period.

All dolls, except the Bisque Limited Edition Dolls, came as either Black or White dolls. Again, with the exception of the 1983 Limited Edition Twin Dolls all of the dolls are marked on the back of the head with the Gerber name and the year they were made.

Plate 41 and 42. show the Anniversary doll in yellow check cloth with rick-rack trim.

Plate 42

Gerber® Baby Dolls
17 Inch Doll in Checked Cloth Body Covering-
Atlanta Novelty
1979 Anniversary Doll Reissued in 1981.

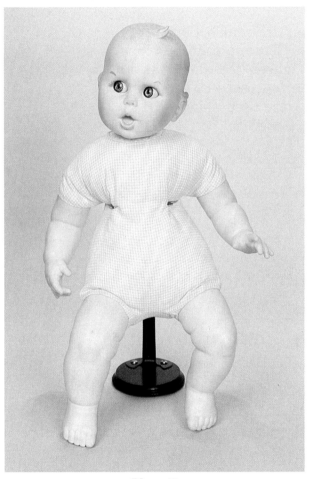

Plate 43

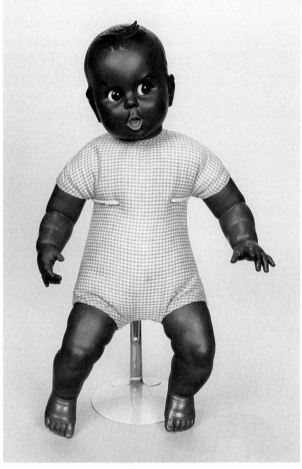

Plate 44

The 1979 17 inch Gerber® Anniversary baby dolls were reissued in 1981. Their bodies were covered with either plain flesh tone colors or checked material the same as the Anniversary dolls. **Plates 43 thru 45** show the reissued dolls in yellow and blue as well as pink and white check cloth.

Gerber® Baby Dolls
17 Inch Doll in Checked Cloth Body Covering-
Atlanta Novelty
1979 Anniversary Doll Reissued in 1981.

Notice there is no rickrack on these dolls. Seldom will you find a reissue doll with checked material and rickrack. When you do I would guess the doll was an Anniversary doll that has been redressed or there may have been some left over that were used along with the reissue dolls.

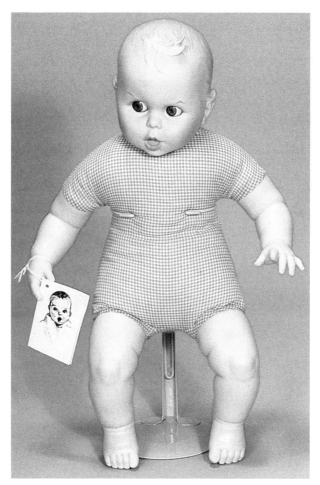

Plate 45

Gerber® Baby Dolls
17 Inch Doll in Checked Cloth
Body Covering with Skirt and Bib.

Plates 46 thru 48. The Anniversary dolls were reissued in 1981. The checked cloth body was dressed in a gingham skirt and bib trimmed in rickrack. All the dolls wore socks on their feet.

Plate 46

Plate 47

Gerber® Baby Dolls
1979 / 1981 Atlanta Novelty

Plate 48

Plate 48A

Gerber® Baby Dolls
Atlanta Novelty reissue in 1981 of the 1979 17 inch Anniversary doll

Plates 49 and 50 show the 17 inch Atlanta Novelty doll reissued in 1981 in a pink check body suit covered with a lacy see-through skirt and bib.

Plate 49

Plate 50

Gerber® Baby Dolls
Atlanta Novelty reissue in 1981
of the 1979 17 inch Anniversary doll

Plates 51 and 52 show the 17 inch Atlanta Novelty Gerber baby doll reissued in 1981 in a blue check body suit covered with a lacy see-through skirt and bib.

Plate 51

Plate 52

Gerber® Baby Dolls
Atlanta Novelty reissue in 1981
of the 1979 Anniversary doll

Plate 53 and 54 show the 17 inch Atlanta Novelty Gerber Baby Dolls reissued in 1981 in a yellow check body suit covered with a lacy see-through skirt and bib. This series of dolls also came wearing little booties tied with matching ribbon.

Plate 53

Plate 54

Gerber® Baby Dolls
Atlanta Novelty reissue in 1981
of the 1979 Anniversary doll

Plate 55. This little sweetheart wears a pink checked, long sleeve dress over her checked body suit. Her detachable bib will keep the spills off her pretty dress.

Plate 56. Baby in Gingham Play-Suit. A Gerber baby doll dressed in a gingham play suit which buttons down the back. The gingham matches the checked body covering.

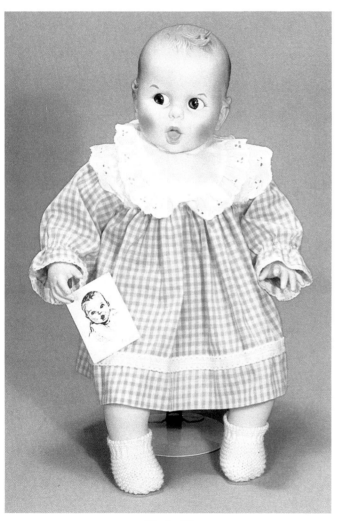

Plate 55

Plate 56

Gerber® Baby Dolls
The 17 Inch Anniversary dolls
by Atlanta Novelty were reissued in 1981.

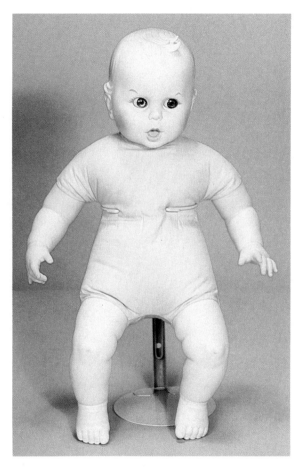

Plate 57

Plate 58

Plates 57 and 58 show undressed dolls in **plain pink or brown cloth body suits**. They are then outfitted in a variety of outfits as can be seen in the following plates.

Gerber® Baby Dolls
1979/81 Atlanta Novelty

Plates 59 - 64 Pajama Gerber baby dolls came with their heads laying on a little pillow which matched their outfit. Dressed in her two piece brushed rayon pajamas, trimmed in ribbon, they are ready for their nap.

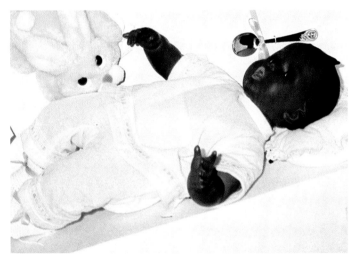

Plate 59
Doll from Jill Nihart Collection

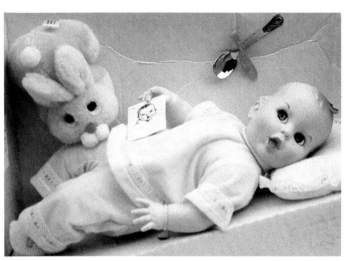

Plate 60

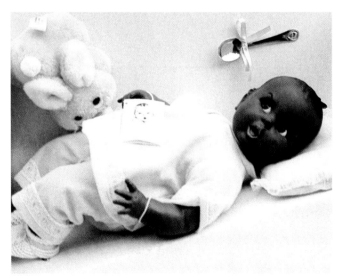

Plate 61

Plate 62

Gerber® Baby Dolls
1979/81 Atlanta Novelty

Plates 63 - 64 Pajama Gerber® baby dolls came in three colors of pajamas. They were packaged in a window box as were most of the Gerber baby dolls. Dressed in a two piece brushed rayon pajama outfit, trimmed in ribbon, they were packaged with a toy and a Gerber Baby silver (stainless steel) spoon.

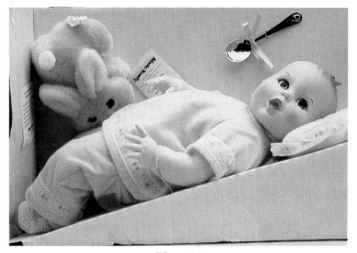

Plate 63

Plate 64

Gerber® Baby Dolls
1979 /1981 Atlanta Novelty

Plate 65

Plates 65 and 66. The 17 inch Gerber Baby Doll with Matching Pillow and Coverlet comes dressed in a flowered bed jacket with matching panties, pillow and coverlet. The polyester filled body is covered in appropriate flesh toned cloth.

White doll courtesy of Jill Nihart

Marked on the back of the neck:
Gerber Products Co.
© 1979

MARKETING: Retail Stores: Cost—$25.75. This cost is based on the price quoted for other dolls in this collection which appeared in the 1980 Summer issue of *Treasure Trove.**

Very hard to find.

* Wank, M.&A., *Treasure Trove*, 1980

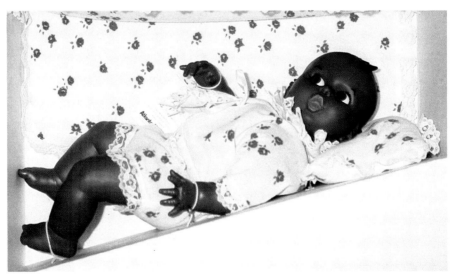

Plate 66

Gerber® Baby Dolls
1979 /1981 Atlanta Novelty

Plate 67

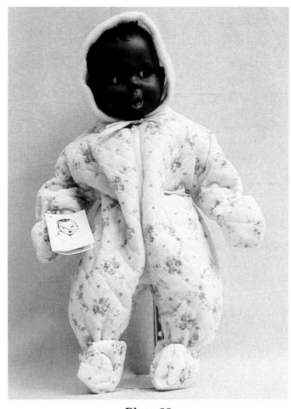

Plate 68

Plates 67 - 68. The 17 inch **Gerber® Baby-Snowsuit** has a removable zippered snowsuit with a matching attached hood which ties with a cord. Like the other reissue Anniversary Dolls the body of these dolls is covered with appropriate flesh toned colored cloth.

White Doll courtesy of Jill Nihart.

Marked on the back of the neck:
Gerber Products Co.
©1979.

Sold through retail stores: Cost: $25.75. This is an assumption, based on the price quoted for two of the other dolls of this series, in the late Summer, 1980 issue of *Treasure Trove*.

Very hard to find

* Wank, M.& A., *Treasure Trove*, 1980.

Gerber® Baby Dolls
1979 /1981 Atlanta Novelty

Plates 69 and 70. This adorable 17 inch baby doll came dressed in a beautiful rose or blue colored velour dress, with white cotton sleeves, and a large matching ruffle at her neck. She has white cotton panties, and white knit booties. The soft cloth body is pink flesh colored on the White doll and dark brown on the Black doll.

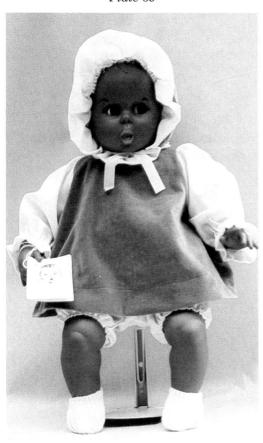

Plate 69

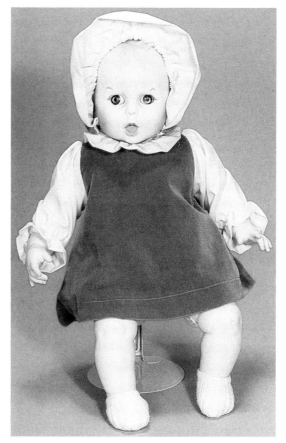

Plate 70

Marked on the back of her neck:

Gerber Products Co.
© 1979

Plate 71

Gerber® Baby Dolls
Mama Voice Doll
1979 / 1981 Atlanta Novelty

Plate 72

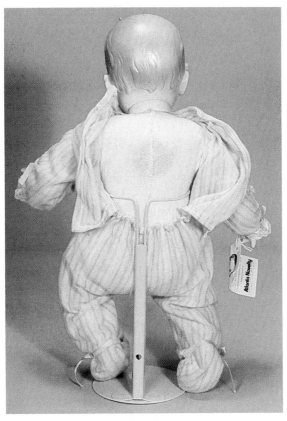

Plate 73

PLATES 72 - 75. The **17 inch** Gerber® Mama Voice baby doll came in two completely different models. In the first version the body is covered in flesh colored cloth, dressed in a stripped sleeper, and packaged with a stuffed teddy bear, two miniature boxes of cereal, and a "silver" spoon. The mama voice box is located in the doll's back as seen in **Plate 73**.

Marked on the back of the neck:

Gerber Products Co.
©1979.

Sold   through   retail   stores: Suggested price was $25.75*

* Wank, M.&A., *Treasure Trove,* 1980

55

Gerber® Baby Dolls
1979 /1981 Atlanta Novelty
"Mama" Voice

Plate 74

Plate 75

Plates 74 and 75. Shown are the Gerber baby "Mama" Voice dolls as they were tied into their packaging. The inner box was packed inside a widow box. The Black doll was also available in blue P.J.'s.

17 Inch Mama Voice Doll
Atlanta Novelty 1979/1981

Plates 76 and 77. In the second version of the **17inch Mama Voice Gerber®️ baby doll** the body is covered in blue and white or pink and white checked cloth, the same as the Anniversary Doll, but with out the rickrack trim. She is dressed in white panties, and different styles of a ribbon trimmed lace dress with matching booties. The pictures show that one is packaged with an extra yellow lace skirt and matching bib while the other comes with blue stripped pajamas and a silver spoon. The mama voice box is located in the chest of some of these dolls instead of the back.

Plate 76

Plate 77

Gerber® Baby Dolls
1979/1981 Atlanta Novelty
17" Cries Mama Dolls

Plate 78 - 81 shows more "Cries Mama" Gerber babies dressed in beautiful eyelet dresses which cover their pink or blue check body covering. They are wearing booties and come packaged with an extra outfit and silver spoon.

Plate 78

Plate 79

Plate 80

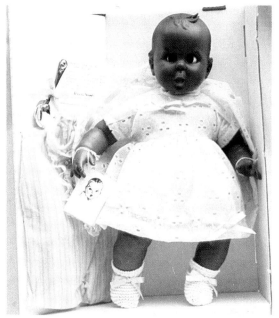

Plate 81

Gerber® Baby Dolls
1979/1981 Atlanta Novelty
17" Drink and Wet Doll

Plate 82 and Plate 83 show the undressed cloth body of the 17 inch **Drink and Wet** doll. Note the opening in the cloth body which allows the water to run through. How does the cloth body handle the wetness?

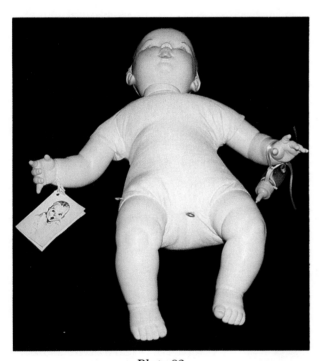

Plate 82

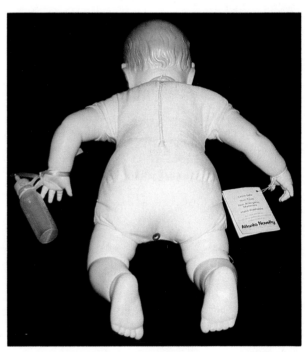

Plate 83

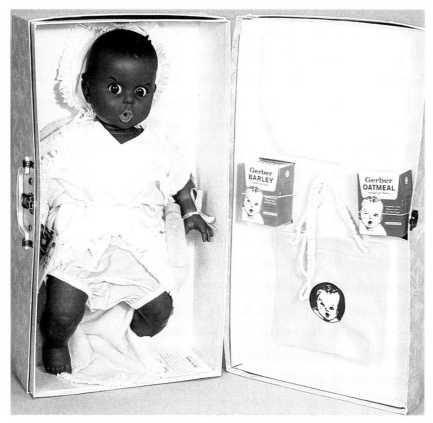

Plate 84

Plate 85

Gerber® Baby Dolls 1979/1981 Atlanta Novelty

Plates 84 and 85. The 17 inch Drink and Wet in Trunk Gerber baby doll comes in a trunk and is dressed in a shirt and plastic pants. She is wrapped in a blanket tied with ribbon. Her accessories include a diaper, diaper bag, baby bottle and two boxes of Gerber Cereal. She is available as a Black or White Baby. Her body covering is the appropriate flesh tone color.

A change in the construction of these 1981 reissues of the 1979 Anniversary doll enables the little mother to feed the baby water and have it wet its diaper. A tube leading from the mouth through the body allows the water to escape through a brass valve.

The author can not help but wonder what happens to the cloth body if it is often subject to moisture. Finding these dolls in mint condition becomes a collector's dream.

Marked on the back of the neck: Gerber Products Co.© 1979

Sold through retail stores: Cost —-$25.75*

*Wank, M & A., *Treasure Trove*, 1980

12 Inch Plain Body Form
Atlantic Novelty Gerber® Baby Dolls
1981 Collector Dolls and 1985 Pinafore Dolls

Plate 86 and 87. The **1981 12 inch Collector Dolls and the 1985 Pinafore Dolls** have soft cloth bodies with vinyl heads, arms and legs. The body of the White doll is made of white material instead of the usual flesh tone pink. Brown cloth is used for the body of the Black baby.

Plate 86

Plate 87

Gerber® Baby Dolls
1981 VINYL COLLECTOR DOLL
Atlanta Novelty

Plate 88

Plate 89

Plates 88 and 89.

Beautifully dressed in a turn of the century eyelet lace christening dress with matching cap, these beautiful **Collector Dolls** are cradled on a matching lace trimmed pillow in a wicker basket. The dress sleeves have satin bows at the wrists, and a satin ribbon adorns her neck. The dress closes in the back with velcro. White knit booties with satin ties and a flannel diaper, which also closes with Velcro, complete the wardrobe. Their bright pink cheeks and rose bud mouth make them a real collector's choice.

Marked on back of Neck:
Gerber Products CO./ ©1981

Sold through retail stores:
Cost, $44.50*

* Wank, M&A., *Treasure Trove*, Spring 1981

Gerber® Baby Dolls
1981 / 1985 Atlanta Novelty

Plate 90. This **12 inch "Little Miss Pinafore"** doll with a soft polyester stuffed cloth body and vinyl head, arms and legs, comes in both Black and Caucasian styles. She is dressed in white tights and T shirt covered by her white rose bud trimmed lace pinafore. A matching white bonnet, also trimmed with rose buds, adorns her beautiful little face.

Plates 91 and 92. Her accessories included either an extra blue dress with matching panties, white knit booties and "Dr. Dentin" type pajamas, or an extra dress, stuffed animal, feeding dish and bottle warmer. She has a bright pink open/close mouth and painted cheeks. Her body form is identical to the 1981 vinyl with soft body doll. However, the neck is marked 1985.

All of the Atlanta Novelty Company 12 inch dolls, were sold through retail stores.

Plate 90

Plate 91

Plate 92

Gerber® Baby Dolls 1981 Atlanta Novelty 12" Drinks and Wets Doll

Plate 93

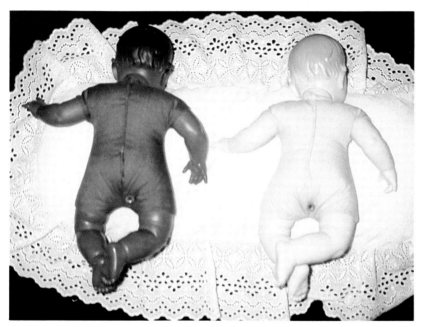

Plate 94

Plates 93 and 94. This **12 inch Drink and Wet Gerber® Baby Doll** has vinyl arms, legs, and head with molded hair and floating eyes. Her soft polyester body is stuffed with shredded polyester and she is surface washable by hand. A tube leads from her mouth to an opening in her body to allow water to drain through. Again the author questions how the cloth body of these dolls was able to resist moisture to keep from rotting. The uniqueness of this design makes these dolls a valuable addition to a collection.

Marked on the back of her neck:
Gerber Products Co.
© 1981

MARKETING: Retail Stores: Cost: $24.99 JC Penney 1981 Toy Catalog, Page 399.

Gerber® Baby Dolls
1981 Atlanta Novelty
12" Drinks and
Wets Doll

Plate 95

Plate 95. One version of the **12 inch Drink and Wet doll** by Atlanta Novelty, distributed by JC Penney Co., comes in a wicker basket lying on an eyelet lace trimmed pillow. A complete layout is included: diaper carrying case, diaper, washcloths, pompoms, dress, hangers, booties, squeeze toy, shampoo, baby oil, plate, bottle, bottle warmer, food boxes, Gerber Baby Spoon. *

Plate 96. The second packaging of the **Drink and Wet doll** came with two teddy bears, one fuzzy and one made of plastic, a feeding dish, bottle warmer, and two terry cloth wipes. These dolls were available as either a Black or White Baby.

Both dolls are dressed in a polyester and cotton flannel crawler suit with pink ribbons .

Plate 96

12 Inch Mama Voice
Atlanta Novelty
1981 Gerber® Baby Dolls

Plates 97 and 98. The undressed views of the **Mama Voice Gerber® Baby Doll** show the location of the voice box which is located in the back of the doll.

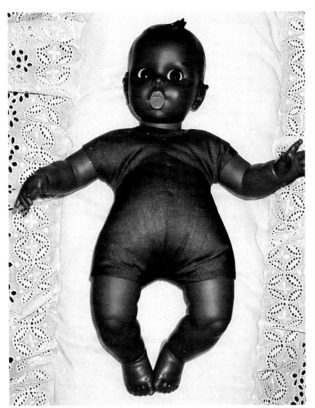

Plate 97

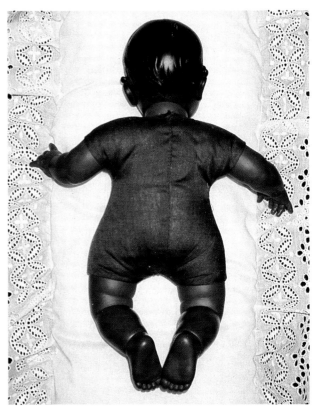

Plate 98

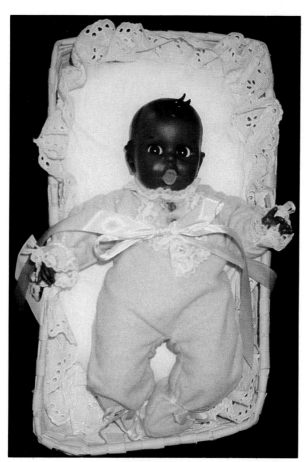

Plate 99

Gerber® Baby Dolls
1981 Atlanta Novelty

Plates 99 and 100. The distinctive feature of this **12 Inch** doll is her **"mama" voice**. She comes dressed in footed pink pajamas. Her wardrobe consists of a lace trimmed dress, matching panties and booties. She is packaged in a window box along with a stainless steel Gerber® Baby spoon*

Plate 101 shows the Black doll wearing the extra dress that came packaged with her accessories.

Marking on back of the neck:
Gerber Products Company
(c) 1981

MARKETING: Retail Stores,Cost: $28.50**

** Wank, M.&A., *Treasure Trove,* Spring 1981

Plate 100

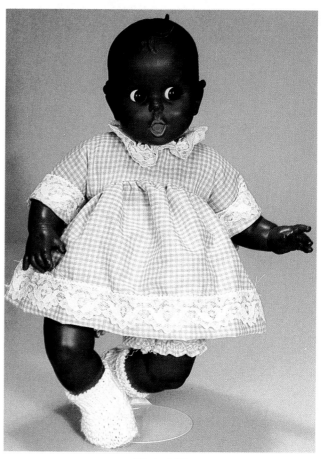

Plate 101

Gerber® Baby Dolls
1981 Atlanta Novelty
12 inch Cries Mama in Baby Carrier

This Gerber baby doll set includes a bonanza of outfits for the darling little soft bodied Gerber baby doll. As can be seen in the picture she comes in a flannel bunting while snugly held in her baby carrier. She comes packaged with a Sunday best dress and diaper as well as an additional 3 piece outfit: T Shirt, tights and jumper. A baby bunny toy completes this set.

Plate 102

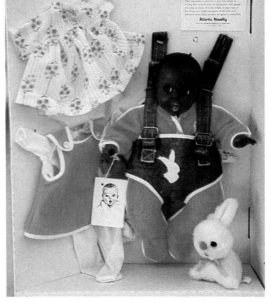

Plate 103

Gerber® Baby Dolls
1985
Atlanta Novelty

Plates 104 and 105. The bodies of the **12 inch and 17 inch Premium Bathtub Gerber Baby Dolls** were made of foam filled vinyl. Their heads turn, and they have the familiar floating eyes that move back and forth. Their one piece foam filled bodies make them wonderful bathtub toys. They are identical except for size.

Marked on the back of the neck:

GERBER PRODUCTS CO.
 (c)1985 (12 inch size)
 (c)1979 (17 inch size).

* *The Gerber Baby Dolls*, Gerber Products Company

Plate 104

Plate 105

12 inch Vinyl Bathtub Baby
Atlanta Novelty 1985   Gerber® Baby Dolls

Plate 106

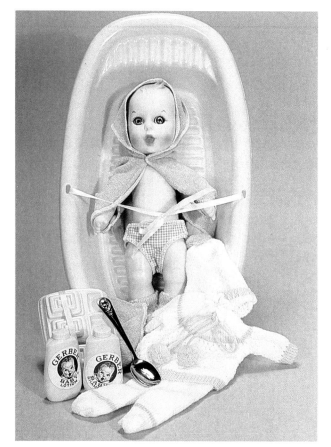

Plate 107

The 12 inch **Bath Tub Gerber® Baby Doll** was available as a **Premium Offer** for $7.95 plus three UPC symbols. ($26.00 retail value)

Offer expired December 31, 1985. 4,432 dolls sold through this offer.*

Plates 106 and 107. Packaged in a window box, the 12 inch vinyl bathtub Gerber baby doll came dressed in a hooded terry cloth towel. A nightgown, diapers, booties and a three piece knit outfit, in either pink or blue, were included. Other accessories were a bath tub, soap dish, washcloth, mock lotion and shampoo bottles and a nursing bottle. However, they are not drink and wet dolls. They were available in both Black or White.

Plate 108 shows the dolls dressed in the dresses that came as part of their accessories.

These basic dolls were also available through retail stores in different packageing. **See Plates 116 and 117.**

*Gerber Products Company Archives

Plate 108

12 inch Vinyl Bathtub Baby
Atlanta Novelty 1985 - Gerber® Baby Dolls

Plates 109 and 110 show the Bathtub babies as they came "tied" in their display boxes. The dolls came in both pink and blue outfits with matching tubs and as Black or White doll babies.

Plate 109

Plate 110

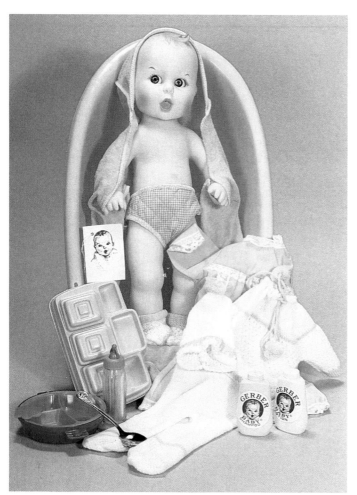

Plate 111

Gerber® Baby Dolls
17 inch Vinyl Bath Tub Baby
Atlanta Novelty 1985

The 17 inch **Bath Tub Gerber® Baby Doll** was available as a **Premium Offer** for $11.95 plus three UPC symbols. 7,200 dolls were sold through this offer. The offer expired in December, 1985. *

Plate 111. The Bath Tub Gerber® baby doll came with quite a wardrobe. Wrapped in a hooded towel, wearing only a diaper and lying in a tub, she is surrounded by her toiletries and clothes. **Plate 112** shows her dress and booties. A three piece knitted snowsuit was packed in her tub along with two mock lotion and shampoo bottles and a magic nursing bottle. A miniature accessory tray and terry washcloth were also included. This doll came as a Black or White doll, in pink or blue, with a matching tub.

* Gerber Products Company Archives

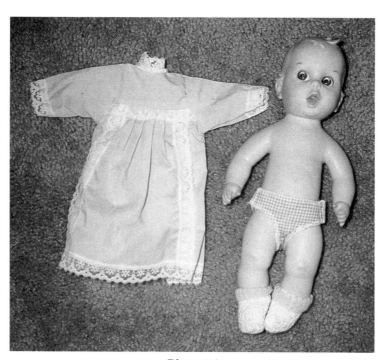

Plate 112

Gerber® Baby Dolls
1985 Atlanta Novelty

17 inch Bath Tub babies as they came tied in their original window boxes.

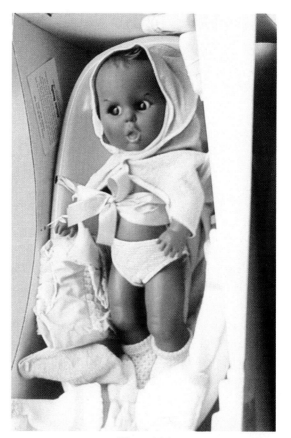

Plate 114

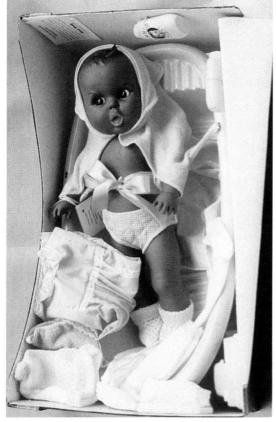

Plate 113

Plate 115

73

Gerber® Baby Doll 1985
AtlantaNovelty
12" Foam Filled Dolls

Plate 116

Plate 116 displays several **12 inch foam filled dolls** designed for the retail stores. These were the same dolls offered as a Premium through Gerber, but in different packageing. These cute little babies can be found dressed in three piece knit snowsuits in various combinations of blue, pink and yellow. One has been found dressed in a little pink bunting, others in a cute little dress that bottons at the shoulders. This doll wears tights and a long sleeve polo shirt. **(Plate 117)** They all came packaged with a small stuffed animal which was also made by Atlanta Novelty. Teddy bears, kittens, dogs, bears and elephants could be found in the packages. Other accessories included were a plastic feeding dish, bottle warmer, a silver spoon, extra outfits, miniature boxes or jars of baby food or baby toiletries. Not all accessories were found with each doll.

These dolls are often found packaged in over sized boxes in which information intended to describe other dolls has been masked out. These dolls were the last ones produced by Atlanta Novelty. Since there appears to be more variety in their packaging than any other group I suspect this production served as a clean-up for odds and ends.

Marked on the back of the neck:
Gerber Products Co.
(c) 1985

Plate 117-Dolls from Ellen
Cappadonia collection

Gerber® Baby Dolls
1984 Atlanta Novelty, Inc.

Plates 118 and 119. The 14 inch Gerber® Musical Dreamy Doll has sleep eyes and a soft plush body filled with poly foam. She has a wind-up music box in her back which plays Rock-a-bye Baby. She is soft and cuddly. It is amazing that any still exist that have not been loved to death. She is included in this section because she has the charming Gerber Baby face. She was available as both a Black or White baby doll, in white or pink plush material.

Plate 120. The 14 inch Musical Dreamy Doll in its original packaging.

Plate 118

*Doll in box
courtesy of Ellen Cappadonia.*

MARKS: Cloth label: Atlanta Novelty / A Subsidiary of Gerber Products Co./ Made in Hong Kong

MARKETING: Retail Stores

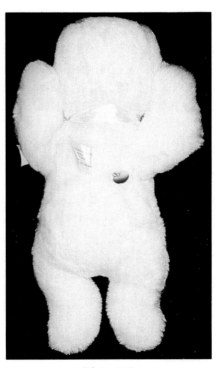

Plate 120

Plate 119

GERBER® BABY DOLLS

1979-1985

MANUFACTURER
ATLANTA NOVELTY

1981-1982-1983

LIMITED EDITION BISQUE COLLECTOR DOLLS

During 1981, 1982, and 1983 Gerber baby dolls were available as Limited Edition bisque collector dolls. Artist Neil Estern, working from the unfinished charcoal drawing of the Gerber Baby done by Dorothy Hope Smith, sculpted the face, arms and legs while the Shader Doll Company crafted the pieces out of very fine porcelain. Atlanta Novelty, a division of Gerber Products Co., produced a 14 inch doll in 1981, a 12 inch doll in 1982 and 10 inch boy and girl twins in 1983. The molds were broken at the end of each year's production.

The bodies of the dolls are made of soft stuffed cloth. Every porcelain bisque piece is dated and the head is numbered. Each head is hand painted and the eyes are cemented into the head. The 12 inch and the 14 inch dolls have the floating eyes, while the 10 inch twins have sleepy eyes that open and close. *

* Press Releases, Atlanta Novelty

Gerber® Baby Dolls
1981- Limited EDITION-PORCELAIN-COLLECTOR DOLL
Atlanta Novelty

Plates 121 and 122. The **14 inch** Limited Edition doll is made with a porcelain head, arms and legs, with a soft body. She has set-in flirty eyes. She is dressed in a white eyelet trimmed christening gown with a matching underskirt. (Two types of eyelet are shown.) It is an authentic reproduction of an ensemble in the 1902 Sears Roebuck catalog. The gown is trimmed with satin bows at the wrists and a satin ribbon at the neck. Her dress is complimented with a matching cap and white knit booties, tied with satin ribbons. She wears a flannel diaper with velcro closure. She comes in a wicker basket lying on an eyelet lace trimmed pillow. Her beautiful baby face is enhanced by the hand painting of her features.*

Marks: Back of neck: Gerber Products /©

Co. 1981: Numbered behind right ear. Arms and legs are dated and marked with initials. The circumference of her head is 11 1/4 inches. This information is included as a reproduction of the Gerber Baby® type head has been made. Although it is not marked "Gerber Products", it bears a striking resemblance to the trade mark head. See section "Look Alike—Look Again".

MARKETING: Sold through direct mail advertisements in national magazines. Cost: Special price to Stockholders, and Gerber Company Employees was $175.00. On the retail market it cost $350.00. Number sold: 10,500. The molds were broken at the end of 1981.

*The Gerber Baby. Gerber Products Company

Plate 121

Plate 122

Gerber® Baby Dolls
1982-LIMITED EDITION-BISQUE-COLLECTOR DOLL
Atlanta Novelty

Plate 123

Plate 124

Plate 123. The **1982 Limited Edition** doll had a porcelain head, arms and legs and a soft body. She has set-in flirty eyes which is characteristic of all Atlanta Novelty dolls except the 1983 Porcelain Twins. She was dressed in white organdy with pink satin ribbon and delicate white lace. Two rows of lace also adorned the pink organdy underskirt. Pink satin ribbon accented the tiny tucked bodice which was also trimmed with embroidered ribbon and lace. She was **12 inches**.*

Plate 124. A close up of the face and dressing of this beautiful doll.

MARKS: Each bisque arm and leg is marked 1982, and the head is numbered.

Marketing: Suggested retail price was $350.00. Gerber Products Company and Shareholders were offered the doll at a special discount price of $175.00 and no maximum purchase order. (*Gerber News*, July-August, 1982.)

Number sold: 5000

The molds were broken at the end of 1982.

* *The Gerber Baby Dolls*. Gerber Products Company

Gerber® Baby Dolls
1983 Limited Edition
Bisque Boy and Girl Twins
Atlanta Novelty

Plate 125

The first Gerber "Twins" were born in 1983. Sculptured by Neil Estern, crafted by Stephanie and Ken Shader and dressed by Mary Cselenyi, these dolls are a Collector's delight. They were introduced that year at the Toy Fair in New York during a special champaign breakfast held in their honor.

Like the 1981 and 1982 porcelain dolls the Twins have soft stuffed bodies with porcelain head, arms and legs.

However, unlike all the other dolls by Atlanta Novelty, which all have the set-in flirty eyes, the Twins have open-close sleep eyes.

Plate 125. The little **Gerber 10 inch twin boy's** outfit of royal blue velvet is trimmed with delicate white lace to complement his organdy and lace shirt front and puff sleeve. Two tiny pearl buttons accent his short knickers, a fashionable beret and white booties trimmed in blue ribbon complete his ensemble.*

(My own doll, which was in its original packaging, did not have the pearl buttons on his knickers, but he is a darling anyway.)

MARKS: Each bisque arm and leg is dated, 1983. Each head is numbered. The marked area is small and the marks are often difficult to read.

* Press release from *Atlanta Novelty*, a Division of Gerber Products Co; 2/11/83.

Gerber Baby Dolls
1983 Limited Edition
Bisque Boy and Girl Twins

Plate 126. The little **Gerber® 10 inch twin girl** is dressed in rich, ruby red velvet. Dainty white lace adorns her bonnet, dress and pantaloons while embroidered pink rose-buds are scattered on her skirt and highlight her bonnet. White booties with tiny ribbon bows add the finishing touch to her outfit.

MARKS: Each bisque arm and leg is dated, 1983. Each head is numbered. The area to mark is small and the marks are often difficult to read.

MARKETING: Direct sales through national advertising. Suggested retail price $290.00 for one doll or $500.00 for the set.*

* Gerber Products Co. - Corporate Library & Archives; 12/07/88.

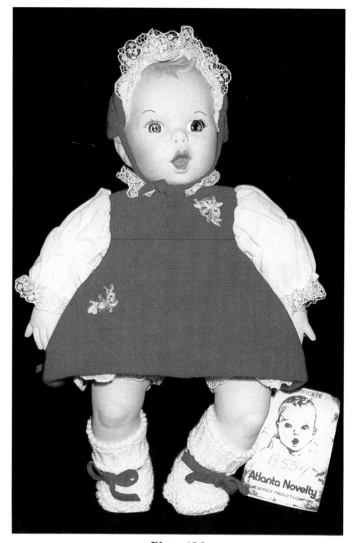

Plate 126

GERBER® BABY DOLLS

1989-1992

MANUFACTURER
Lucky Ltd.

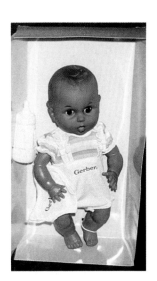

Lucky Ltd. made the Gerber® baby dolls from 1989 to 1992. All dolls carry the 1989 date except the 21 inch doll which is dated 1990. The dolls were made in the 6 inch, 11 inch, 14 inch, 16 inch, and 21 inch sizes. They were made of all vinyl or a soft body with vinyl head, arms and legs.

In addition to the name and date marked on the back of the neck, the 6 inch and 11 inch all vinyl dolls have the Lucky Ltd. logo inscribed on the back of the body. The 14 inch, the 16 inch, and the 21 inch dolls have cloth labels sewn into the seam of their soft bodies which identifies them as being made by the Lucky Ltd. Company.

Gerber® Baby Dolls
1989-1992 Lucky Ltd.

The 6 inch Gerber baby doll, made by Lucky Ltd., is the smallest of the Gerber Baby family of dolls. Made of vinyl, only her head is movable. She has been found as a black baby as well as a white baby, dressed in pink or blue.

Plate 127 shows the dolls dressed in rompers with an attached bib which ties in the back.

Marked on the back of the neck:
© 1989 / Gerber Products Co.

Inscribed on the doll's back:
© 1989 Lucky Inc. Co., Ltd. / Made in China

The Lucky Rabbit Logo is below the printing.

MARKETING: Retail stores.

Plate 127

Lucky Ltd.
1989-1992
Gerber® Baby Dolls

Plates 128 and 129. The undressed views of the smallest of all Gerber® baby dolls is a cute little chubby baby with good detail. Note the Lucky rabbit logo on its back.

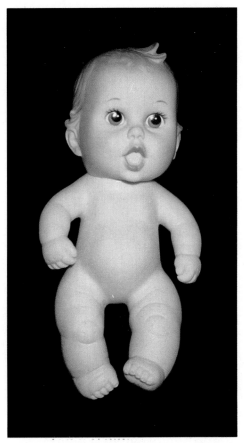

Plate 128

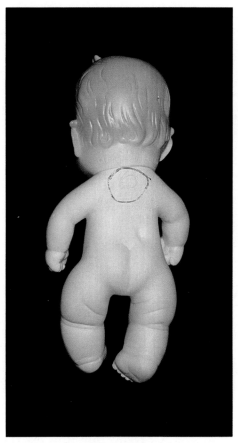

Plate 129

6 Inch Birthday Twins
Lucky Ltd. 1989
Gerber® Baby Dolls

Plate 130. The Gerber® Birthday Baby Twins come packed in a white and blue Gerber® box with several accessories: a play suit with matching bonnet and booties, a plastic birthday cake, an invitation card, a growth chart and a present. One Twin is dressed in a sunsuit with

Plate 130

"Gerber®" written on the bib, and the other in a short pants one piece romper which says "Gerber®" on the front. **Plate 106** also shows one of their friends modeling the extra outfit.

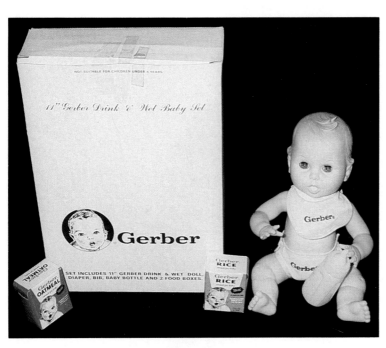

Plate 131

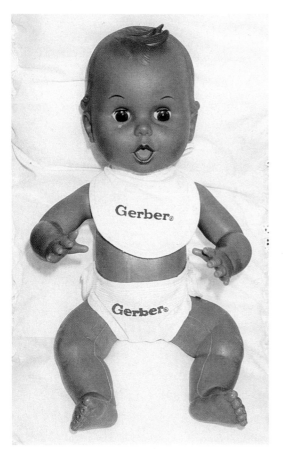

Plate 132

Gerber® Baby Dolls
1989-1992 Lucky Ltd.

Plate 131. The **11 inch Drink and Wet** Gerber baby doll from Lucky Ltd. has a firm vinyl body with a moveable head and sleep eyes. The legs and arms are also moveable. It comes boxed in a set that includes a diaper, bib and baby bottle, all marked Gerber. Two Gerber® baby food boxes are included.

Plate 132 shows the Black doll in her original outfit.

MARKS: ©1989 Gerber Products Co. In addition, each doll's head is marked with a number which appears below the copyright.

The rabbit symbol trademark which spells LUCKY is inscribed on the doll's back.

Sold through Retail Stores.

11 Inch Vinyl Drink and Wet Lucky Ltd. 1989 Gerber® Baby Dolls

Plate 133

Plate 133 The doll also came dressed in a blue and white romper suit with an attached stripped T shirt. Gerber® is printed on the front of the romper.

Plate 134 shows the undressed back view. In this view you are able to see the Lucky rabbit trademark as well as the Gerber copy right on the back of the doll's head.

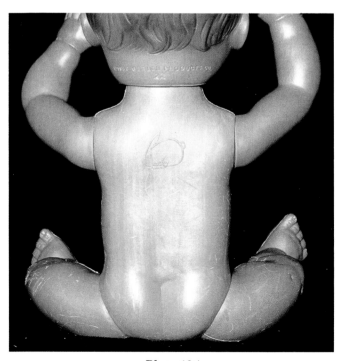

Plate 134

Gerber® Baby Dolls
1989-1992 Lucky Ltd.

Unlike the 6 inch and 11 inch Gerber baby dolls made by the Lucky Company in firm vinyl, the **14 inch** doll was soft and cuddly. It had a soft, cloth body with vinyl head, arms and legs.Its arms are fixed upwards. Its head can be turned. It has an open/closed mouth and sleep eyes. Peculiar to this doll are its adorable little feet. Its big toe is flexed upwards and slightly outwards. Undressed bodies can be seen in **Plates 135 and 136**.

A cloth label sewn to the body has the Lucky name and trademark, and additional information.

MARKETING: Retail stores.

Marked on back of neck:
© 1989 Gerber Product Co.
"All Rights Reserved"

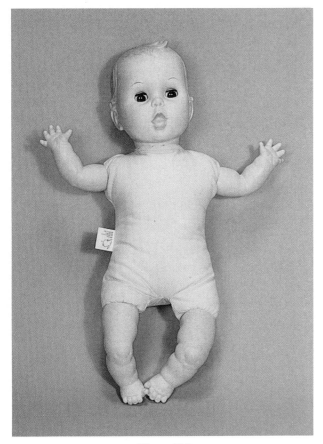

Plate 135

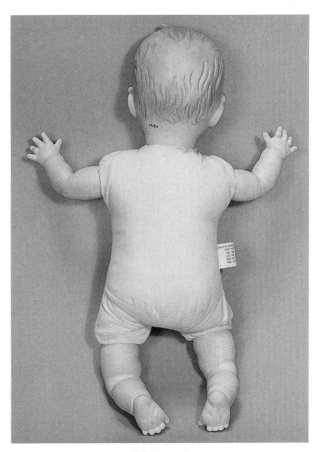

Plate 136

Gerber® Baby Dolls
1989-1992 Lucky Ltd.
14 inch Vinyl with soft body

Three different models of the doll are shown here. **Plate 137** shows the **14 inch Baby Doll Traveler Gift Set**. Her set includes the pink and white, or blue and white romper suit, with matching hat and booties, a passport, boarding pass, and a postcard.

Plate 138 shows the doll dressed in a long white christening gown. Her **Gerber Baby Gift Set** includes two miniature boxes of Gerber cereal, 2 plastic jars of Gerber strained vegetables, a plate and training cup with a Gerber Baby transfer on them. A spoon, baby bottle and a toy are also included.

In **Plate 139** the **Soft Body Doll** is dressed in a little two piece seersucker outfit which makes it look like a little boy doll. All dolls are very huggable.

Doll from Marian Hart collection.

Plate 137

Plate 138

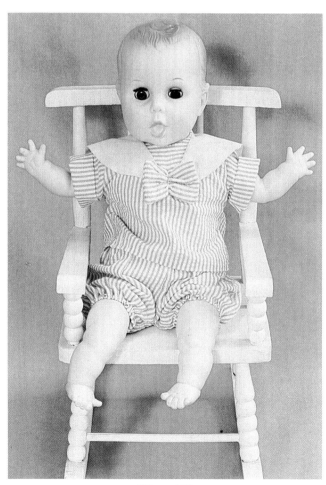

Plate 139

Gerber® Baby Dolls
1989-1992 Lucky Ltd.
16 inch Vinyl with Soft Body

Plates 140 and 141. Just like the 14 inch Lucky Ltd. doll, the **16 inch** Gerber® baby doll is soft bodied with vinyl head, arms and legs. The noticeable difference, besides size, is the molding of the hands and feet. The hands of this doll have been made in a delightfully delicate real baby-like form. These dolls also have sleep eyes. Like all Gerber baby dolls they have a rose bud shaped mouth with a molded tongue.

Marked on the back of the neck:
©1989 Gerber Products Co.
"All Rights Reserved"

A cloth label sewn to the the body has the Lucky name and trademark, and additional information.

Marketing: Retail Stores.

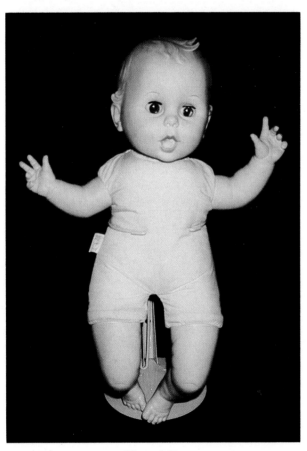

Plate 140

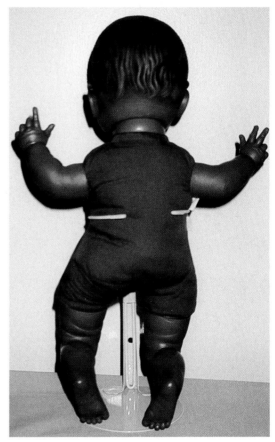

Plate 141

16 Inch Vinyl with Soft Body
Lucky Ltd. 1989
Gerber® Baby Dolls

Plates 142 and 143. These dolls came dressed in a long white christening gown. The dresses vary in design and material. One MIB doll also had on a bib.

Plate 142

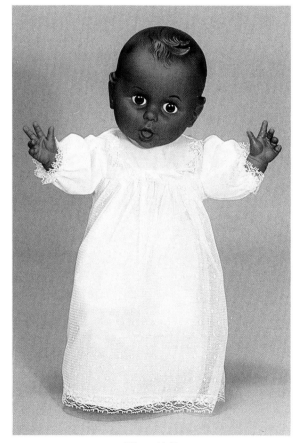

Plate 143

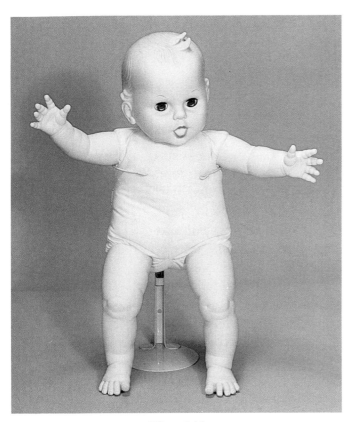

Plate 144

Gerber® Baby Dolls
1989-1992
Lucky Ltd.

The pictured **21 inch** Lucky Ltd. Gerber® baby doll is the tallest of the Gerber® baby dolls. Shown undressed in **Plates 144 and 145**, the doll apears to be life size and beautiful. With outstretched vinyl arms, fingers extended, she is begging to be picked up.

Plate 146. The doll is dressed in red flannel pajamas with a lace trimmed attached bib marked "Gerber". The baby will soon want to close its sleepy blue eyes for the night.

Marked on the back of her neck:
(c) 1990 Gerber Products Co.
"All Rights Reserved"

A cloth label has the Lucky Ltd. name and trademark, plus additional information.

MARKETING: Q VC

A Black version of this doll has not been identified.

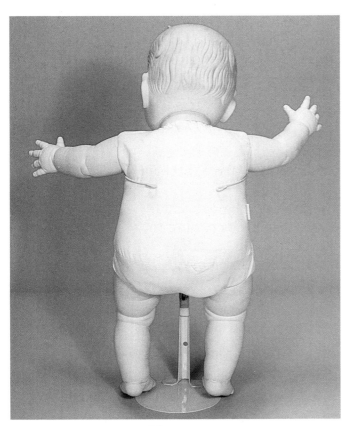

Plate 145

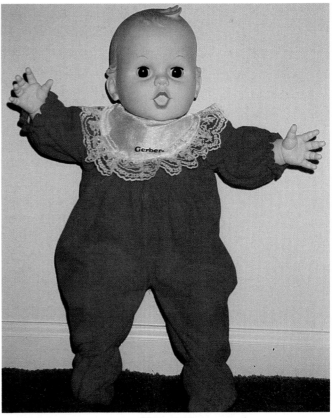

Plate 146

GERBER® BABY DOLLS
1994-1996
TOY BIZ, INC.

In 1994 Gerber Products Company began a licensing agreement with Toy Biz, Inc. of New York. Ari Arad, leading toy inventor and CEO of Marvel Films, worked with the Gerber staff to develop the new line of life like dolls, produced by Toy Biz, Inc., for the 1994 and 1995 retail markets*. Of this group, all the dolls carry 1994 as the date on the back of the neck except the 1995 Gerber® Newborn Baby™ doll with sleep eyes. All other Toy Biz dolls have painted on eyes. Dolls with soft bodies carry a label on them which further identifies them as either 1994 or 1995 editions. Dolls with all vinyl bodies have no further identification than the mark on their head .

The dolls can be divided into four separate groups. The first group consists of six dolls. It is called the Complete Gerber® Nursery (1994-1995) and is promoted as a child's first nurturing doll. An unique feature of this group is the addition to the head of a vinyl hair "top knot". The second group, Gerber® Growing Toys, introduced the Gerber® Talking Baby™ doll (1994-1995). Besides the three versions of the talking dolls, the group included two additional dolls. The third group, the Gerber® Newborn (1995), had three dolls. The last group, the Gerber® Collector dolls (1995), has three dolls.

In April, 1996 Toy Biz introduced its latest dolls; the Gerber® Fruit Babies™, in both the Black and White versions. This is a sweet smelling bunch! For the 1996 Holiday Season the latest of the talking dolls, the Gerber® Alphabet Talking™ Doll, will make its debut.

All the dolls come in a window box with the particular doll's name and accessories listed on the box. Depending on the color of the doll the box shows the doll as either African American, Hispanic or White. All dolls come with their own storybook to provide communication between child, doll and parent.

MARKETING: Retail Stores.

* Kutz, K. Cuddly. *Gerber Baby Dolls*, <u>Doll World</u>, 1995

Gerber® Baby Dolls
1994 Toy Biz, Inc.
Gerber® Nursery™ Dolls

Plate 147. Gerber® POTTY TIME BABY™ made of all vinyl comes dressed in a white print dress trimmed in aqua, an aqua diaper and white booties. A large baby bottle is attached by pink ribbon to the bow of her dress. She is 15 inches long.

Marked on the back of the neck
©1994 Gerber Products Co.
Toy Biz, Inc.

MADE IN CHINA: Marked on doll's back.

Plate 147

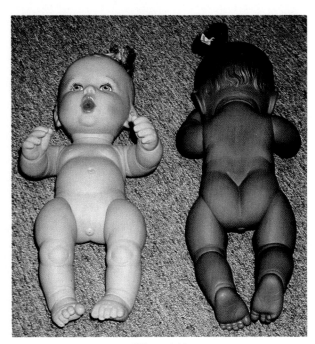

Plate 148 displays the undressed body of this doll. Note the little body creases and folds characteristic of a new baby. The nipples, navel, and wetting hole add to make this doll very realistic.

Plate 148

Gerber® Baby Dolls
1994 Toy Biz, Inc.
Gerber® Nursery™ Dolls

Plate 149. Gerber® TUB TIME BABY™ is made of firm vinyl and comes dressed in a pink terry cloth robe trimmed in blue and white poke-dot binding, with a matching headband. A plastic yellow duck is attached to her wrist by a pink ribbon. The doll is 15 inches long.

Plate 150 displays the undressed body of this doll. Note the little body creases and folds characteristic of a new baby. The nipples and navel add to make this doll very life like. These dolls have painted-on eyes.

Marked on back of head © 1994 Gerber Products Co. TOY BIZ, INC.

Marked on doll's back: MADE IN CHINA

Plate 149

Plate 150

Gerber® Baby Dolls
1994 Toy Biz, Inc.
Gerber® Nursery™ Dolls

Plate 151

Plate 151. LOVING TEARS BABY™ has a firm vinyl head, arms and legs with a soft body. She comes dressed in a white print dress with pink trim, and matching bonnet and panties. A velour teddy bear and a large plastic baby bottle are attached to the front of her dress by pink ribbons. She is 15 inches long.

Marked on back of neck :
© 1994 Gerber Products Co.
TOY BIZ, INC.

Plate 152

Plate 152 shows the front and back of this doll. The attached cloth label reads: Gerber and Baby Head® / © 1994 Toy Biz, Inc./ Made in China.

Gerber® Baby Dolls
1994 Toy Biz, Inc.
Gerber® Nursery™ Dolls

**Plate 153. Gerber® FEEL BET-
TER BABY™** has a vinyl head, hands
and feet. Her foam stuffed, cloth body
is dressed in a non-removable hooded
sleeper. A stethoscope is included for
the heartbeat sound. The doll is 15
inches tall.

Marked on back of neck:

MARKS: (c) 1994 Gerber
Products Co.
TOY BIZ, INC.

Attached cloth label reads

Gerber and BABY HEAD (R)
(c) 1994 TOY BIZ,INC.

Made in China

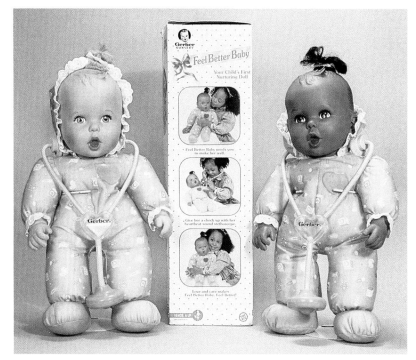

Plate 153

1994-1995 Toy Biz, Inc.
Gerber® Nursery ™ Dolls

Plate 154

Plate 154. Made of firm vinyl with a top knot of hair, the 15 inch **GERBER® FOOD TIME**™ DOLL comes packaged with her own food dish, a play jar of Gerber® applesauce and a magic spoon which makes it look as if the doll is actually eating as it is being fed. She is dressed in a one piece "shorts" play suit with attached bib. She is wearing white socks on her feet. **She has the same vinyl body as the Tub Time Baby.**

©1994 Gerber Products Company / TOY BIZ, INC.

Plate 155

Plate 155. A Special Edition of this doll was made and sold exclusively through Kay Bee Toy Stores. It was called **Gerber® Food & Playtime Baby**™. Additional accessories included a baby bottle, an extra outfit, and a rubber duck tethered to the doll's wrist. A food dish was not included. A cloth label attached to her play suit identifies this doll as being a trademarked Gerber® Baby Doll made by **Toy Biz, Inc.** in 1995.

Gerber® Talking Baby©
Toy Biz, 1994
Gerber® Baby Dolls

Described as the "Gerber® Baby that talks and grows with your child", these beautiful, delightful high tech dolls come as a boy or girl doll, in Black, White (1994) or Hispanic (1995). They wear a pink or blue non-removable soft velour and cotton print pajama, as seen in **Plates 156, 157 and 158**. The girl doll has a matching pink velour headband while the boy doll wears a blue velour half cap. They have soft bodies with vinyl head, hands and feet. Marking:

©1994, Gerber Products Co.
TOY BIZ, INC.

The dolls have three levels of learning. On level 1, by touching any one of eleven parts (Ears, eyes, mouth, nose, hands, feet, or tummy) the doll will say the name of the part. On level 2 the doll will repeat any of the eleven parts plus add a phrase (Hands, "Hands\, Hold my hand"; Feet, "Feet, Tickle my feet",: Eyes, "I see you"; Nose, "Nose, Smells good!"; Mouth "Mouth, Tastes Good!"; Tummy, "Tummy", and the doll giggles. Level 3 has the doll playing "Follow Me". By touching any three body parts the doll will repeat each one in turn. The dolls have sweet little child voices and are fun to play with. These dolls are sold through retail stores.

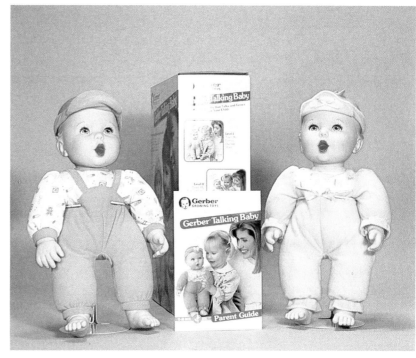

Plate 156

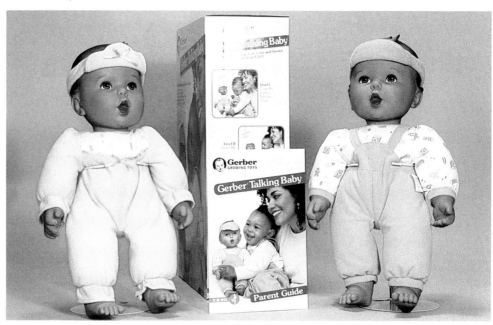

Plate 157

Bilingual Hispanic/American
Gerber® Talking Baby™
Toy Biz, Inc. 1995

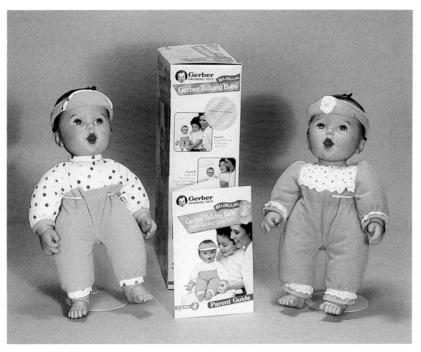

Plate 158

Plate 158. The 1995 Gerber Hispanic Talking dolls say the same things in both Spanish and English as the 1994 White and Black Talking dolls say only in English. The cloth label on the doll's body identifies it as being made in 1995. The head is marked 1994. All the dolls in this group are 14 inches tall. They have painted on eyes.

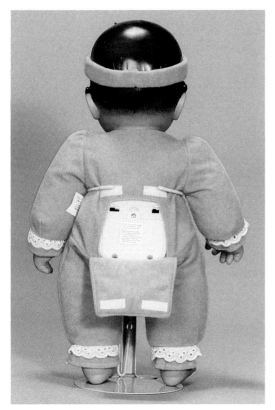

Plate 159

Plate 159. The computer box for the voice is located under the drop seat of the doll's non-removal clothes.

Gerber® Baby Dolls
Toy Biz, Inc. 1994
Gerber® Growing Toys™

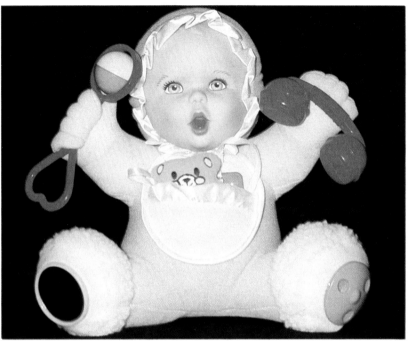

Plate 160

Plate 160. GERBER® PLAYTIME™ BABY is described as "Baby's First Playtime Activity Friend" . The 15 inch doll is made with a vinyl face and painted eyes. It has a soft body and is dressed in a non-removable velour play suit with matching cap. Different textures and colors are used to stimulate the child's sense of sight and touch. The pocket of its non-detachable bib holds a squeaky teddy bear and a teether. Additional accessories include a telephone rattle attached to its left hand, a spinning ball rattle attached to its right hand, a turning dial, located on the sole of the left foot which makes a ratchet sound and a mirror attached to the sole of her right foot.

Marks: Attached cloth label reads

Gerber and BABY HEAD®
© 1994 TOY BIZ,INC.

MADE IN CHINA

Gerber® Baby Dolls
1995 Toy Biz, Inc.
Gerber® Growing Toys™

Plate 161

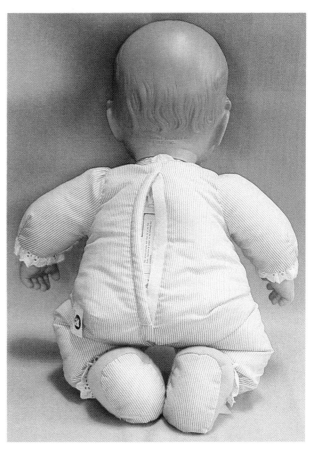

Plate 162

Plate 161. The Gerber First Sounds Baby Doll coos, cries, and giggles just like a real baby. Fitted with three AAA batteries (not included) she begins to cry when her hand is squeezed. But when picked up and loved she coos and giggles. The soft cuddly body is covered in soft cotton material. The head and hands are made of vinyl.

Plate 162. The opening for the batteries can be seen in this view of the doll's back.

Marked on the back of the neck
1994 Gerber Products Co.
Toy Biz, Inc.

The body has a cloth label which says

Gerber and Baby Head (R)
TM and (c) 1995 Toy Biz, Inc.
New York, N.Y. 10076
All Rights Reserved Made in China

A picture of the Gerber Baby is also on the label.

Gerber® Baby Dolls
1995 Toy Biz, Inc.
Gerber® Newborn™Dolls

Plate 163

Plate 163. GERBER® NEWBORN BABY™ DOLLS are cuddly **13 inch** snuggle babies. Much like a real newborn these dolls need to have their heads supported when they are picked up. Made of soft stuffed velour with sleep eyes they can suck their thumb. Their removable caps, with permanently tied bows, fasten with velcro. Available as Black or White baby.

MARKS: (1995) GerberProducts — Marked on back of neck TOY BIZ, INC.

Cloth label on body reads:
Gerber and Baby Head ®
TM and (c) 1995 Toy Biz, Inc.
New York, N.Y. 10076
All rights Reserved Made in China

A picture of the Gerber Baby is also on the label.

Gerber® Baby Dolls
1995 Toy Biz. Inc.
Gerber® Newborn™ Dolls

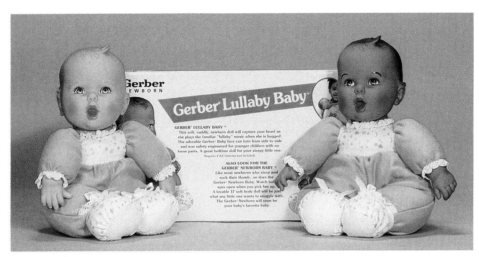

Plate 164

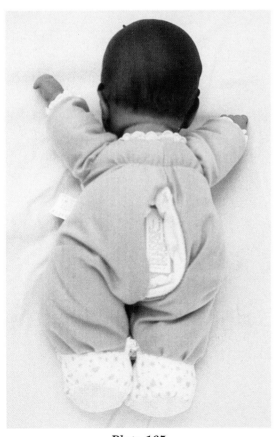

Plate 165

Plate 164. The **Gerber® Lullaby Baby** ™ doll is basically the same doll as the Gerber Twins. The difference is the computer box in the Lullaby Baby's back which can be seen in **Plate 165**. The doll is charming, soft and cuddly. When she is picked up to be hugged she plays Brahms Lullaby. Her head, like that of the twins, is smaller than the other vinyl heads with painted on eyes. It seems to fit the short 11 inch body much better. The doll is available as both a Black or White doll.

Marks: Also, like the Twins, the writing on the back of the neck is unreadable. A cloth label on the body identifies the doll as a trademarked product of Gerber Products Company, made by Toy Biz, Inc. 1995.

Marketing: Retail stores.

Gerber® Baby Dolls
1995 Toy Biz, Inc.
Gerber® Newborn™ Dolls

Plate 166. The 13 inch **Special Edition Gerber® Twins**™ have the same body as the Lullaby Baby except no music box is embedded in its back. Their soft, huggable bodies are covered in colorful velour. Only their hands and head are made of vinyl. A plastic bottle marked Gerber® is attached to their sleeve. Where-as the Newborn Baby has sleep eyes, the Twins have painted on eyes. The upper part of the eye is painted a darker shade of blue than the bottom portion. The heads of the Twins are smaller than the head of the First Sounds Baby.

Marks: The markings on the back of the heads are not legible.

A cloth label on the body identifies them as trademarked Gerber Baby dolls made by Toy Biz, Inc. in 1995.

Plate 166

Made exclusively for Kay Bee Toys, Inc.

Gerber® Baby Dolls
Toy Biz, Inc. 1995
Collector Dolls

Plate 167

Plate 167. "As a Timeless Tribute to the World's Most Respected Baby Face"*, Toy Biz, Inc.recognizes the multi-cultural emphasis in education today by producing their 1995 Gerber® Baby **Collector Dolls** as Black, White, or Hispanic babies. To achieve this difference they have made the Hispanic doll a little lighter shade of brown than the Black doll.The Collector Dolls are **17 inches tall**. They have soft bodies with vinyl heads, arms and legs. They come dressed in lace trimmed satin christening dresses. Each of the three dresses varies a little in design. Each doll has matching satin slippers with little crossed laces. Her white under panties are made of cotton. The packaging includes an "individually numbered Certificate of Authenticity printed on special paper"*, and a booklet titled Collector Doll- Parent Guide.

The dolls were designed to be played with, "or to be a child's first introduction to special dolls and doll collecting. Their beautiful classic features and durable construction resemble a real porcelain doll."*

Marked on the back of her neck:
(c) 1994 Gerber Products Co.
TOY BIZ, INC.

Marketing: Retail Stores- The dolls, planned for the 1995 Holiday Season, became available in retail stores in early November, 1995. The ethnic dolls were generally only available in selected markets. In October the Sears Wish Book featured the White doll. *Toy Biz, Inc.

Gerber® Fruit Babies
Toy Biz, Inc. 1996
Gerber Baby Dolls

Plate 168

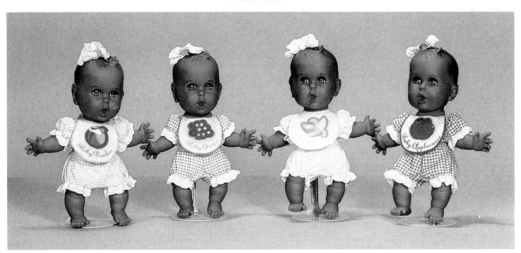

Plate 169

Plates 168 and 169. The **Gerber® Fruit Babies**™ have the adorable Gerber baby face and a real fruit smell. 8 inches tall, these four little dolls are made with a soft stuffed body and soft vinyl head, arms and legs. They have painted on blue eyes, wide open palms on their out - stretched hands, and little curly toes. They are dressed in a one piece, lace trimmed, removable play suit. The matching hair bow is attached to the doll's head by a plastic heart. The color of the suit corresponds to the color of the fruit. Their sewn on bib has a plastic picture of a piece of fruit which is the same as the name on the bib. The very fragrant smell comes from the plastic bib, I think. The little cuties are called (and smell like) Baby Grapes, Baby Applesauce, Baby Peaches, and Baby Bananas.

Gerber® Alphabet Baby
Gerber Baby Dolls
Toy Biz, Inc. 1996

Plate 170. The Gerber Talk 'N Learn™ Alphabet Baby Doll sings the alphabet song when its hand is squeezed. It has three levels of learning. On the first level it sings the ABC song. On the second level it omits letters so the child can fill in the blanks. On level three it plays only the music so the child can test his/her memory skills and sing along. As with all Toy Biz talking dolls it requires 4 "AA" batteries. The doll's computer has an automatic turn off. The doll is available as either a Black or White doll.

ITEM NO.24216

Plate 170

Plate 170-A

Plate 170-A. Baby Care Set from the Gerber Nursery line of Toy Biz dolls. 1996. The set includes: Bib, Bonnet, Receiving Blanket, Food Jar, Bottle, Magic Spoon, Food Dish and Tethered Bear.

©1996, Gerber Products Co.
TOY BIZ, INC.

LOOK ALIKE-LOOK AGAIN!!

The old saying among Antique people , "Fool me once -shame on you! Fool me twice, shame on me!", holds true when searching for Gerber® baby dolls. Armed with enough knowledge of what marks to look for the buyer can avoid being fooled even once.

As you will remember the head of each Gerber® baby doll is marked with the name Gerber® in some form. All dolls, except those made by the Sun Rubber Company (Viceroy/Sunruco Co., Canada) between 1955-1958, are also marked with the date. I found my first "look-alike" at an antique show in Centerville, Michigan. Although the dealer did not try to pass it off as a Gerber doll, she thought it might be. Since it had nothing inscribed on the neck, I knew it wasn't. The vinyl head resembles the Gerber® baby head made by Lucky Ltd. in 1989. It could have fooled the unknowing buyer. The unmarked doll has very long unattractive eyelashes. The body, arms and legs are not in correct proportion. A cloth label says it was made in Hong Kong for Yuletide Concepts Inc. N.Y. The back of the tag reads Stuffed Toys/ Ohio. I paid $10.00 for this doll so I could take its picture. (Plates 171 &172)

My second purchase was in the category of "Fool me once"! This time I was delighted that I had found the 13 inch Sun Rubber doll at a reasonable price. (I should have been alerted when the dealer came down to $20.00.) I recognized the familiar face and markings on the back of the neck right away. Since I have both the 10 inch and 18 inch dolls I quickly grabbed up my new purchase and went out the door to the car. Just as when I was a little girl, I quickly undressed her. Something was wrong! The body, which was in a full PJ outfit with only the hands showing when I bought her, was most strange. I turned her over to look for the Sun Rubber name and patent numbers. As hard as I looked they didn't appear. Only then did I real-ize that the Sun Rubber doll head had been put on a vinyl unmarked body. See **Plates 173 and 174**. The arms and legs of this doll are almost straight, more like the 18 inch Sun Rubber doll. However, **Plate 12** shows that the legs of the 13 inch doll are bent like those of the 12 inch doll. My second clue should have been when I saw that the doll did not have sleep eyes as did the original 13 inch doll. **Plate 13**.

But the story doesn't end there. Whereas, I thought this doll was just a poor reproduction, it may not have been. In talking with Ed Mobley, (see Sun Rubber Co., 1955-1958) he told me that it was not unusual for doll companies, left with a supply of heads, to put them on a generic body, repackage them, and sell them through the retail market. This may be true of this doll. The fact remains it is not the original 13 inch Sun Rubber doll shown in their ads.

An 11 inch doll's head made by Lucky Ltd., was found on a body which was much too small for the head **(Plates 175-176).** Since all vinyl bodies on Lucky Ltd. dolls I had seen were marked with the Lucky rabbit logo, I guessed that this doll was another example of a head on the wrong body. The short body of this doll simply says "Made in China". However, I have now found three of these dolls all dressed alike in little blue terry cloth outfits. This doll may have been offered through the Visitor Center at the Gerber Products Company in 1989. After those experiences I deliberately set out to look for "clones". Unfortunately, I didn't have to look long.

Since the Gerber® Baby head is a registered trademark reproducing it without permission is illegal. Plate 178 shows the undressed form of the 1981 porcelain Gerber® baby doll. Several examples of attempts to reproduce the porcelain Gerber Baby doll head have been found. **Plate 179** shows a reproduced unmarked porcelain head with painted-on eyes, and porcelain arms and legs, on a most unattractive cloth body. **Plate 182** shows a doll dressed in a long white christening gown which looks a lot like the original gown in which the 1981 Gerber porcelain doll came dressed. I have come across many all porcelain look - alike Gerber dolls. Some of these dolls are being sold by dealers as unmarked Gerber® baby dolls. Most of the dolls have painted on eyes. Some have glass or plastic inset eyes. **Plates 183 and 188**. The original Gerber dolls, that are being copied, have set-in flirty eyes, or sleep eyes like the 1983 porcelain Twins. Most of these reproduction dolls are beautifully dressed. However, **Gerber® baby dolls were never made with porcelain bodies nor did the porcelain dolls have painted on eyes.**

Another find was an Arrow doll (1965) whose sleep eyes had been replaced with set in eyes. I didn't buy that one. The dealer was asking $75.00!

My latest find is a 9 inch all porcelain doll

Gerber Baby
Magnet
See Part II
Plate 53

with set-in plastic eyes. **Plates 186-187**. She came dressed in the white christening outfit, basket and eyelet pillow, which belongs to the 12 inch 1981 Collector doll. I paid $55.00 for this doll just to be able to take its picture. The dealer also had a 14 inch, all porcelain, reproduction "Gerber" baby doll with glass eyes dressed in a beautiful blue and white christening gown. She wanted $185.00. Of course I didn't buy it. I prefer to put my money into an original Gerber® doll than a reproduction.

Collectors should be concerned about reproduction or altered Gerber® baby dolls. No matter how cute they may be they are not the original. I paid $165.00 for the first all porcelain reproduction. I knew it was a repro when I bought it, but I needed it for pictures. Ignorance is not bliss when it comes to the pocketbook. Producers of molds and people who make them and sell them as Gerber® baby dolls are doing so illegally. The buyer is the loser. So, Buyer Beware!!

Look Alike - Look Again !

Plates 171 and 172. The unmarked soft body doll with a vinyl head is placed next to a Gerber® baby doll by Lucky Ltd.

Notice the similarity of the head hands, and feet. Take away the long eye lashes on the unmarked doll, the heads become almost identical.

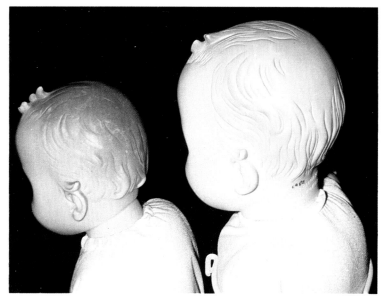

Plate 171

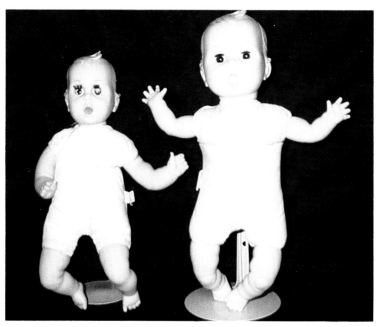

Plate 172

Look Alike - Look Again !

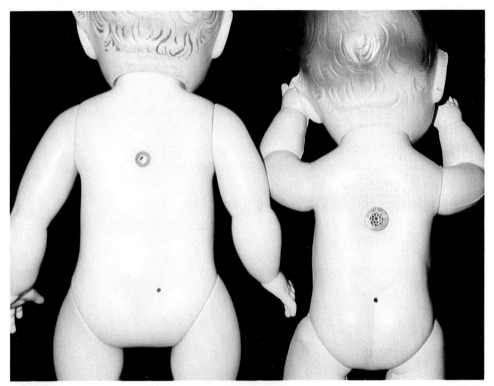

Plate 173 13" Sun Rubber Company head on a generic body. Notice the lack of identification on the body of the doll on the left. The doll on the right is the real Sun Rubber Doll.

Plate 173

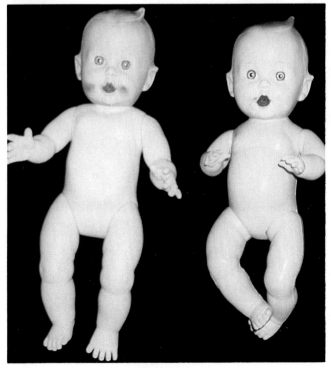

Plate 174 The un-dressed front view shows the straight arms and legs of the generic body instead of the bent arms and legs like those of the 12 inch Sun Rubber doll on the right. Also, the 13 inch Sun Rubber had sleep eyes. See **Plates 12 and 13**.

Plate 174

Look Alike - Look Again !

Plates 175 and 176. The Lucky Ltd. company put the Gerber Baby head on an all vinyl body marked "Made in China". Usually when the head for their 11 inch doll appears on a vinyl body the body is clearly marked with the Lucky rabbit logo. Since the author has found three of these dolls it is assumed that they were made for a specific market and were intended to be that way. These dolls measure about nine inches overall and come dressed in a terry cloth, one piece outfit with lace trimmed patch pockets, which fastenes in front with velcro.

I have recently found this doll MIB which says it is 11". I believe it was put in this box at the last minute.

Doll courtesy of Ellen Cappadonia

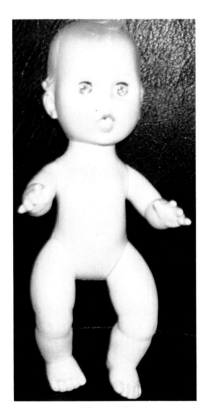

Plate 175

Plate 176

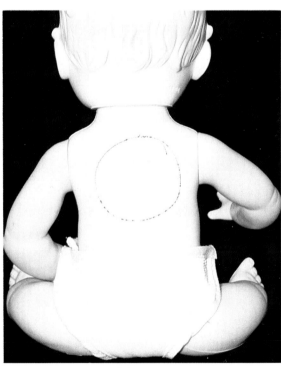

Plate 177

The Lucky Ltd. trademark shows clearly in **Plate 177**.

Look Alike - Look Again !

Plate 178 shows the undressed form of the 14 inch Special edition, porcelain with soft body, Gerber® baby doll made by Atlanta Novelty Company in 1981. Several reproductions of this head, minus the flirty eyes, have been found by the author. Some are marked Gerber® and some are not. **Reproducing the Gerber® baby head, in any form, without the expressed permission of the Gerber Products Company, is illegal.**

Plate 179. An attempt at reproducing the 1981 porcelain with soft body, Gerber® baby doll has resulted in a rather comical looking doll. Clothes, understandably, make a big difference. This reproduction has painted on eyes, but the typical open/close mouth of the original doll.

Doll from Ellen Cappadonia collection.

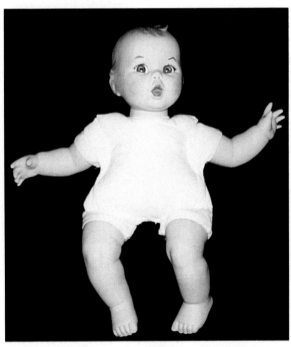

Plate 178

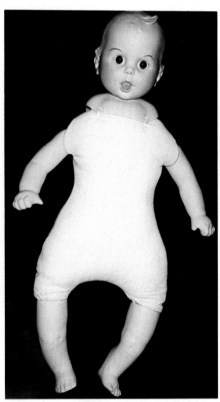

Plate 179

Look Alike - Look Again !

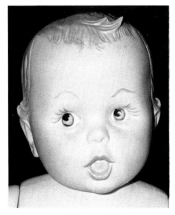

Plate 181

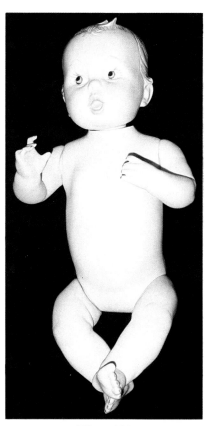

Plate 180 shows the undressed form of an all porcelain 14 inch Gerber® baby doll look-alike. **Plate 181** shows a close-up of the doll's face. There are no markings on this head.

Plate 182. This same doll is dressed in an eyelet outfit much like the original 1981 Special Edition Gerber® baby doll.

Plate 183 shows a beautifully dressed look-alike all porcelain doll with beautiful glass eyes. It is marked Gerbert Doll by Dudy / # 23 / 1992. Notice the spelling of this name. This was done, supposively, to keep from infringing on the registered trademark. *(Doll from the Barbara Maxson collection)*

Plate 180

Plate 182

Plate 183

Look Alike - Look Again !

Plates 184 and 185. These plates show the undressed form of an all porcelain 9 inch Gerber® baby look-alike doll. This doll is marked D & J.C on the back of the neck. **The Gerber® baby doll was never made with an all porcelain body.**

Plate 184

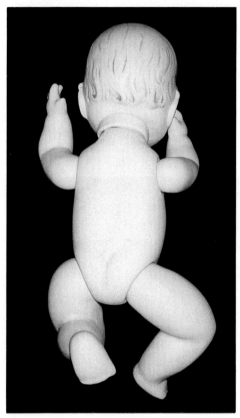

Plate 185

Look Alike - Look Again !

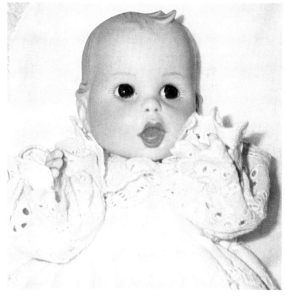

Plate 186

Plate 186. A close-up of the 9 inch Gerber® baby Look Alike. She has brown in set eyes. The original dolls have blue inset eyes.

Plate 187 shows this doll dressed in the original clothing of the Atlanta Novelty 12 vinyl Gerber® baby collector dolls. See Plates 88 and 89.

Plate 188 Another beautiful Gerber Baby doll look-alike. Dressed in a tan colored long lace dress her glass set-in non-moveable eyes resemble the flirty eyes of the Atlanta Novelty dolls. She is unmarked.

Plate 187

Plate 188

PART 2
GERBER®
ADVERTISING
COLLECTIBLES

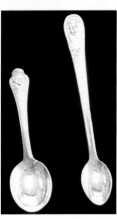

Gerber Advertising Collectibles

Gerber Products Company first began to issue premiums back in the early 30's. These first premiums included baby blankets, feeding dishes, cups, bath thermometers, toys, etc. The most famous premium was the Gerber baby cloth girl or boy dolls issued in 1936 for ten cents and 3 Gerber baby food labels. The next most sought after premium is the 1941 silver plate spoon, made by Winthrop Silver, a division of International Silver Company. The Gerber baby head shapes the top of the spoon. It was available for twenty-five cents and 6 Gerber labels or box tops. All premiums were discontinued from 1941 -1946 because of World War II. The spoon offer was renewed in 1946 and continued until 1956. It was revised at that time. This time the Baby head® was embossed into the handle. Oneida Silver also made the spoons beginning 1972 (See "Spoons" in the Collectibles list).

The first baby food label featured the brand name Gerber's at the top of the label . Three tumbling building blocks were in the center of the label and the variety name of the product was at the bottom of the label followed by the word "unseasoned". On January 1, 1929, the label was approved by the United States Patent Office. In preparation of an advertising campaign the Company ran a contest for a suitable baby picture to go along with the ads. In 1928 Dorothy Hope Smith submitted a charcoal drawing of her friend's baby, Ann Turner (Cook). The picture was accepted without revision and became the registered trademark on June 12, 1934. (For further information see *A Brief History of the Gerber Products Company*, and *The First Gerber Baby—A Real Living Doll*. Also, refer to the bibliography listing, <u>History of the Fremont Canning Co. and Gerber Products Company- 1901 to 1984.)</u>

Collecting Gerber Products Company memorability can become a real challenge, but the results from persistent searching can be very rewarding. Gerber did not do mass merchandising of collectibles for the sake of the Collector as many companies have done. Instead, the Collector should ask advertising dealers for items with the Gerber® name or / and the Gerber Baby picture on them. Items produced before 1994, at which time Sandoz of Switzerland bought the Company from the stockholders, are considered to be the most collectible.

Collectible items will fall into several main categories: premium items: toys, dishes, spoons; Commemorative items, like things from the 25th and 50th anniversary celebrations and sponsored events; freebies from the salesmen and through the Company Visitor Center or tours like books, pamphlets, pictures, cups, spoons etc.; special recognition awards, rewards, honors, and contest items of one kind or another; employee related work items, like clothing, uniforms and tools; paper items such as magazines ads, books and pamphlets, calendars, visitor center passes, brochures and stock holder gift notices etc; Gerber Corporate Identity items, adult and children clothing, sports equipment and numerous other items. The corporate identy program, which began in 1978 with eleven items, offers over 100 items to employees and retirees in 1996. The earlier items are beginning to appear on the secondary market and are highly prized by the collector.   Happy Hunting!

Plate 1 Baby Care/Wear

SH.H.HH! Baby's Asleep! Of the three signs, the one on the right is the oldest. It dates to the **40's**. The signs were available by writing to Gerber. The sign on the left is a cut out and has an attached 15 cent store coupon. It was available in **1972. 1954** is given as the date for the third sign.

(Plate 1)

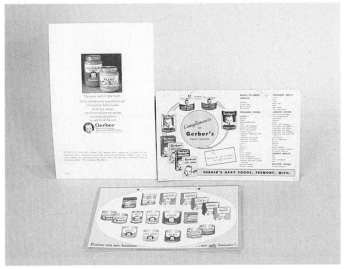

Plate 2 Baby Care/Wear
The backs of the signs in Plate 1 carry Gerber advertising. The signs measure approximately 5" x 8".

(Plate 2)

(Plate 3)

Plate 3 Baby Care/Wear
Gerber Disposal Wash Cloths came in a 4 1/2 "x 41/2" x 1 1/2 " box. Advertised as " New for baby / and you / 25 / Gerber Disposable / Wash Cloths". Has Gerber Baby head on package. Circa. **1971**. This marked the end of the slogan *"Babies are our business... our only business. "Our only business"* part of the slogan would be dropped in **1970** as Gerber added Junior Foods to their foods line. *From the Shirley Brooks and Bob Johnston collections*

Plate 4 Baby Care/Wear
Gerber Baby Travel Kit. The set contains 3 sample bottles of Gerber Baby Oil, Shampoo, and Lotion plus an instruction sheet on how to refill the bottles. Circa. **1988**.

(Plate 4)

Plate 5 Baby Care/Wear

Baby Thermometer designed to be used in a baby's bath. On reverse side from the scales is a picture on the Gerber Baby and the words "Foods for Baby". 3" long. Circa. **1938-39**. This was a **premium** item which was available by sending in 5 cents and 3 labels from Gerber® baby strained foods.

(Plate 5)

Plate 6 Baby Care/Wear

Back side of bath thermometer. **1938-1939**.

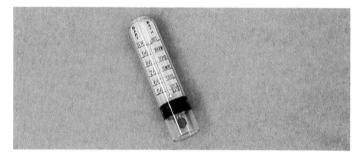

(Plate 6)

Plate 7 Baby Care/Wear

Gerber® Babywear Department Sign. This 12" x 34' printed sign has an applied paper Gerber Baby head decal. Advertising signs are rare and considered to be a real find. Circa. **1965**.

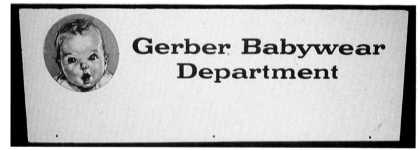

(Plate 7)

Plate 8 Baby Care/Wear

Gerber Babywear Gift Set included a plastic bib, vinyl pants, pull-on undershirt and stretch socks packed in a plastic tote bag with snap fit handles. All items marked Gerber. **1980**.

Photo from Gerber Archives.

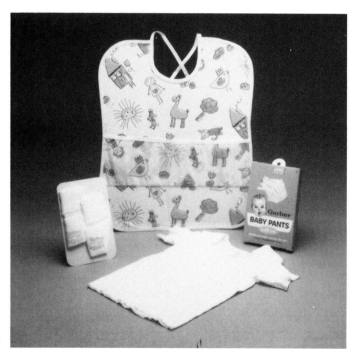

(Plate 8)

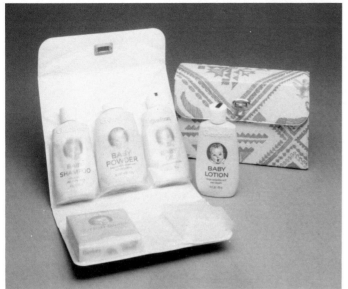

Plate 9 Baby Care/Wear
Gerber Infant Care Product Kit. 1980.
The kit included a travel case with 4-ounce bottles of Gerber lotion, baby oil, powder, shampoo and a package of 54 cotton swabs.
Photo from Gerber Archives.

(Plate 9)

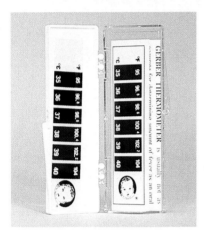

Plate 10 Baby Care/Wear
Baby Fever Thermometer in a plastic case. Pictures of the Baby head are pictured on the contents of the case. Circa. **1990's.**

(Plate 10)

Plate 11 Baby Care/Wear
From the left: **Fire Alert Decal**. This red sticker is known to Fire Fighters and other emergency personnel. Blue and White **Refrigerator Magnet**, and blue **Jar Opener. 1990's.**
Photo from Group II Communications.

(Plate 11)

Plate 12 Baby Feeding Time/Spoons
Blue Plastic Baby Bottle with nipple . The bottles are shaped to look like a penguin and a kitten. The underside is marked "Gerber". **1970's**.

(Plate 12)

Plate 13 Baby Feeding Time/Spoons

Plastic Baby Bottle and Graduate Drinking Cup decorated with pink and blue hearts. Baby head and "I'm a Gerber Baby" are printed on each piece. Circa. **1990**.

From the Bob Johnston collection.

(Plate 13)

Plate 14 Baby Feeding Time/Spoons
Plastic tumblers with the Gerber Baby face screened on one side. The reverse side reads, Babies are our business...our only business! / Gerber ® Baby Foods/ Fremont, Michigan. Circa. **1950's**.

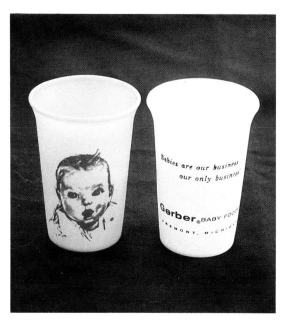

(Plate 14)

122

(Plate 15)

(Plate 16)

(Plate 17)

(Plate 18)

Plate 15 Baby Feeding Time/Spoons

Embossed Plastic Tumblers. 3 1/8" tall, 2 1/4" across top. Available in pink, blue, yellow, and green.The name GERBER and the Baby head are embossed on the surface. "Gerber Products Co. / Fremont, MI. 49412 U.S.A." Circa. **1971.** Earlier tumblers were marked "Made in USA" .

Plate 16 Baby Feeding Time/Spoons

Plastic Bowls (4 1/2" dia.) **with Tumblers.** Available in a variety of colors. Embossed on underside of bottom "Gerber / Baby Foods/ Gerber Products Co. Fremont, MI 49412 / Made in U.S.A. Circa. **1971.**The set was a **premium** item available from the Company for $.50 and a box top from a Gerber cereal with fruit.

Plate 17 Baby Feeding Time/Spoons

Two handle **Training Drinking Cup** with "Gerber" embossed on the lid. Circa. **1990's.**

Plate 18 Baby Feeding Time/Spoons

Gift Set of 24 Jars of Strained Gerber Baby Foods. Circa. **1940's.** *Photo from Gerber Products Company Archives*

Plate 19 Baby Feeding Time/Spoons

Gerber Baby® Can Cover. 2 1/4" diameter. 3 metal can covers were packaged in a Klick-Lok carton and sold through grocery stores for $.10 a package. Circa. **1955**.

(Plate 19)

Plate 20 Baby Feeding Time/Spoons

Silver Spoons marked "Winthrop SilverPlate/ Gerber" (Winthrop was the trademark name used by International Silver for special order items). The 4 1/4" spoon, with the shape of the Gerber Baby head forming the end of the spoon, was a **Premium** offer in **1941** and available for $.25 and 6 Gerber baby food labels. Because of the war the spoon was not made again until **1946**.

It was redesigned and reissued with the 5 1/2" long spoon from **1957 to 1972**. Either spoon was available for $.25 and 6 labels or cereal box tops. The 5 1/2" spoons in this design have been found with the following markings: Winthrop Silverplate , Winthrop Silverplate IS; International Stainless and Wm. Rogers. (See Oneida Spoons). All are marked Gerber.

Plate 21 Baby Feeding Time/Spoons

Silver Spoons marked Gerber/ ONEIDA. Second revised spoons from **1972 to 1996**. Short spoon ,4 1/2". Long spoon, 5 1/2". Note the change of the size of the Baby head and the framing around it. These spoons are often issued as **premiums** with special dates engraved on them. In 1972 they cost $.75 for stainless steel and $1.00 for silver plate, plus 3 Gerber labels or box tops.

(Plate 20)

The author has not been successful in locating a Gerber Baby silverplate spoon made by Oneida. However, **Oneida bought the WM. Rogers Silver Company** in **1929**. A 5 1/2" Gerber Baby silverplate spoon maked Wm. Rogers has been found. It is identical to the 5 1/2" Winthrop spoon except for the name embossed on the back of the spoon.

The author believes these must be the Oneida silverplate spoons refered to in literature from Gerber. They are rare.

(Plate 21)

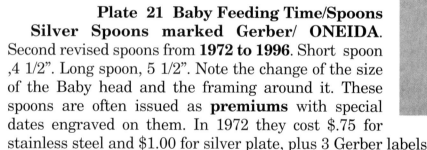

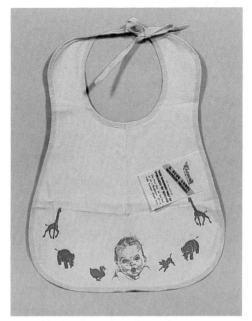

(Plate 22)

Plate 22 Baby Feeding Time/Spoons
Rubber Bib with pink trim. The Gerber Baby and animals are printed in blue. By Kleinerts. Label assures that the garment may be sterilized by boiling. Circa. **1936-1939**.

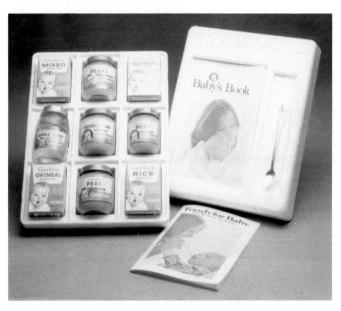

(Plate 23)

Plate 23 Baby Feeding Time/Spoons
Gerber Food Gift Set consisted of a selected assortment of strained foods, cereals and juices packed in a sturdy styrofoam container. The Gerber booklet *"Foods for Baby"* and a silver spoon with the Gerber trademark embosed in the handle were included. These sets were available to stockholders, employees and retirees. 1980.

Photo from Gerber Archives.

(Plate 24)

Plate 24 Baby Feeding Time/Spoons
Gerber Cereal Quads-Free samples of Gerber Cereal Food, followed by Oatmeal, Barley and Rice were offered by writing to Mrs. Dan Gerber in care of the company. See May, 1952, ad following the Collectibles section of this book. The first free sample of cereal was offered in the **early 40's.**

These little boxes were reproduced in **the 70's** and say *"Babies are our business..."* The original sample boxes, which were sent as free samples, say *"Babies are our business...our only business"*.

125

Plate 25 Banks and Cans

Gerber Baby Food Commemorative Banks. The first two –Gerber Strained Peas– cans have blue and white paper labels with a picture of the Gerber Baby and *"Gerber 1928-1978-Fifty Years of Caring"*, plus other information. Circa.**1978.** This label was used from 1928-1938 when the ABC blocks were eliminated and a large picture of the Gerber Baby appeared in the center of the label against a blue rectangle

(Plate 25)

Gerber® Orange Juice Can Banks. Printed on the top surface of can # 3: Be Thrifty / Bank / The / Difference / Buy / GERBER / in / Safety Cans. Circa. **1980**. Lithographed juice cans replaced paper labels in **1955**. These two cans appear together with paper labels in the November, 1941 magazine ad following the collectibles.

Plate 26 Banks and Cans

Candle Can made to look like an early can of Gerber strained peas. The real can had blocks but not the Baby head. The later cans that had the blocks also had a small picture of the Gerber Baby on each block. This can was made in **1992** and is 3" in diameter. A story of the Gerber Baby is on the side of the can.

(Plate 26)

Plate 27 Books, Records

Two outstanding books about the history of the Gerber Products Co. **The Story of An Idea**. This booklet was published in **1953** in connection with the Company's 25th Anniversary celebration. **History of Fremont Canning Co. and Gerber Products Company 1901-1984** is a summary of Corporate annual reports. Another book printed in **1978**, *Fifty Years of Caring*, (not pictured) is a pictorial history of the development of the company. It is hard to find.

(Plate 27)

Plate 28 Books, Records

An assortment of early publications. *Feeding Your Baby* was written in several languages. 1988. *Recipes for Toddlers,* 1952. Both of these booklets were free from Gerber. *The Gerber Sampler of Family Recipes* was available in **1982**.

From the Bob Johnston collection

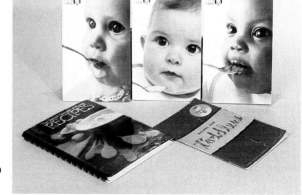

(Plate 28)

Plate 29 Books, Records

Early free booklets. *Bringing Up Baby*, **1972**; *500 Questions New Parents Ask, 1982; Baby Book*, from the **1930's**. The video, *Baby Spoons*, **1988** was given to doctors.

The Story of Jenny Rebecca, was used in training programs for salesmen. Circa. **1964**. It was not for sale to the general public.

From the Bob Johnston collection

(Plate 29)

Plate 30   Books, Records

What is a Baby? In **1958** Rosemary Clooney narrated a beautiful poem which was accompanied by a delightful musical background. This very popular 33 1/3 record was recorded by Columbia Records for Gerber Products Co. and was available as a **Premium** offer.

From Marian Hart collection.

(Plate 30)

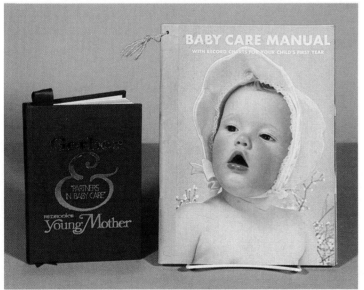

Plate 31   Books, Records

Red Book's *Partners in Baby Care*, 1978. Parents Magazine's *Baby Care Manual* with article titled, " The Baby Foods Box". A picture of baby Dan Gerber, Jr. is featured in the article on page 41. **1943**.

Partners from Bob Johnston's collection

(Plate 31)

Plate 32 Clothes, Personal Items

Man's **Tie** with Baby heads (**1982**), **Baseball cap** with Gerber and Baby head and Webbed **belt** with Gerber repeated six times.

Tie from Lois Witte collection.

(Plate 32)

(Plate 1)

Plate 33 Clothes, Personal Items
Baseball cap in pink with tropical design, 'Gerber' and the Baby head. Issued to promote the new line, Tropical Fruit Products. Circa. **1980's**

(Plate 34)

Plate 34 Clothes, Personal Items
Ski Hat of knitted Dupont orlon acrylic with pom-pom. The hat is dark blue and white with the Gerber logo. **1978**. A Gerber Corporate Identity item.

Model: Barb Stoll; Photo by Loren Hart

(Plate 35)

Plate 35 Clothes, Personal Items
White triangle shaped scarf with "Gerber Baby Food" printed in blue. A tiny picture of the Gerber Baby is worked into the G of Gerber. **1965**.

Plate 36 Clothes, Personal Items
Graduate cap- White twill cap with Gerber Graduates logo, and **Golfer's Cap** with Gerber Baby face screened in blue.**1990's** .

Photo: Group II Communications

(Plate 36)

Plate 037 Clothes, Personal Items (Lower left)
White Scarf with blue Gerber Baby heads,**1978**. (Back left), **Golf Towel**, and **T-shirt** with Gerber and Baby head screened on front .

From the Kyle Converse and Bob Johnston collections.

(Plate 37)

Plate 38 Clothes, Personal Items
Heavyweight Sweatshirt features Gerber Baby face screened full chest and **Graduate Sweatshirt** features a 6 color imprint of the Gerber Graduate logo. **1990's**.

Photo from Group II Communications.

(Plate 38)

Plate 39 Clothes, Personal Items
T Shirt with picture of Gerber Baby on front of shirt. White with blue trim at neck. Made by Health Knit.

(Plate 39)

(Plate 40)

Plate 40 Clothes, Personal Items

Toddler T Shirt with picture of Gerber Baby screened on front of shirt with the words, 'World's Best Known Baby'. Made by Jog Togs. Circa. **1982**.

Plate 41 Clothes, Personal Items

White golf sweater with a picture of the Gerber Baby and the name "Gerber" on the upper left side. **1980's**. *From the Matt Okkema collection.* **Square white scarf** with "Gerber Baby Foods" printed on it.**1950's** These scarfs were worn by the women working on the production line. In the 50's they changed to a triangle shape of lighter material. See Plate 35.

From the Kyle Converse collection.

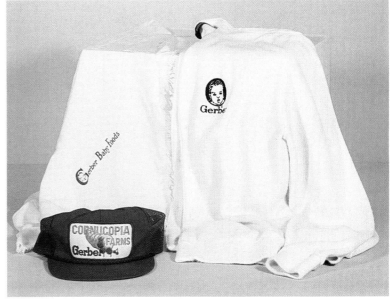

(Plate 41)

Plate 42 Clothes, Personal Items

T-shirts for adults and children. **1978**: Adult sizes and children's sizes. Gerber Baby head in upper left hand corner of shirt.

Photo from Gerber Archives

Plate 43 Clothes, Personal Items

T-shirt with all over print of Gerber Baby face, and **Gerber Graduate T-shirt** with logo screened full chest. **1990's**.

Photo from Group II Communications

(Plate 43)

(Plate 44)

Plate 44 Clothes, Personal Items
Knitted Shoe Mittens. 1984. Gerber printed on each mitten.

From Bob Johnston collection.

(Plate 45)

Plate 45 Clothes, Personal Items
Convenient Travel Kit- with everything you need for overnight in miniature.; **1986.** Gerber is printed on the case.

(Plate 46

Plate 46 Clothes, Personal Items
Roll up T-shirts with Gerber screened over a large G. **1990's.**

Photo from Group II Communications

(Plate 47)

Plate 47 Gerber Corp. ID Items
Gerber® Metal License Plate. 1981; Gerber® and the Gerber Baby head are printed on the plate.

Photo from Gerber Archives.

(Plate 48)

Plate 48 Gerber Corp. ID Items

Swiss Army Knife, Gerber screened in silver, **1986**. **Mag-Lite** is 3 inches long and weighs less than an ounce, packaged in a gift case. Gerber logo is screened in white; **Brass Key Chain** with black logo. Circa **1990's**

Photo from Group II Communications

(Plate 49)

Plate 49 Gerber Corp. ID Items

Square acrylic **Key Tag** with Gerber Baby face; **Graduates Key Chain** with Gerber Graduates logo 6 color design; **Ice Scraper** with Gerber name in black ; **Flashlight Key Tag** with Gerber name in white; **Luggage Tag** -black with Gerber in gold. Circa. **1990's**

Photo from Group II Communications

(Plate 50)

Plate 50 Gerber Corp. ID Items

Sun Visor with Gerber and Baby face.

From Robert Robart collection.

Plate 51 Gerber Corp. ID Items

Clippers and knife in brown pocket holder marked 'Gerber /Baby Foods', **1980's**. **Shoe shine applicator** in plastic case marked' Gerber', **1975 Emery board** with 'Gerber' and Baby head. **Tooth -brush holder** made of soft , white plastic with 'Gerber'. **1980's**.

    Rubber jar opener marked, 'Gerber / Safety Pays'. **Peek through layout viewer** for salesmen and store managers marked 'Gerber', **1985**. **Bandaid dispenser** marked 'Stamp Out Accidents at Gerber/**1977**". **Funnel**, marked 'Gerber for Safety' with a thumbs -up cross. Plastic **Magnifying glass** marked 'Medical Marketing Services'.

From the Bob Johnston collection.

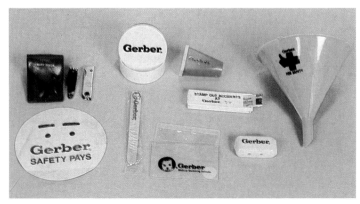

(Plate 51)

(Plate 52)

(Plate 53)

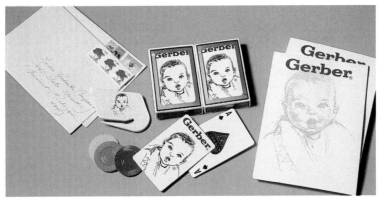

(Plate 55)

(Plate 56)

Plate 52 Gerber Corp. ID Items

A group of **Key Chains** with Gerber and the Baby head. The **two chains** on the left are **gold in color with the design in blue**. A banner which reads 'Gerber Precious Care' flies over a shield with a letter G .The Baby head is in it. The **white chain with the Baby head** also has the message on the reverse side.

Gerber Baby black leather key chain with "Your Key To Growth". The **Gerber Graduate chain** on the bottom right is done in 6 colors.

From collections of Shirley Brooks, Bob Johnston and Bob Robart.

Plate 53 Gerber Corp. ID Items

Refrigerator Magnets.The Gerber Baby Magnet is 1 3/4" in diameter. **1980's Gerber ® Toyline magnet, 1980's**. **Baby food jar** shaped magnet with Gerber Baby face, reads, "Gerber Products Company/ Sensory Evaluation/Test Panels/ Call 1 800 991 3388. 1990's

From the Bob Johnston and Bob Robart collection.

Plate 54 Gerber Corp. ID Items

Grill scrapper. A thumbs-up symbol emerging from a cross has "Gerber" above the symbol and "For Safety" below. **1980's**

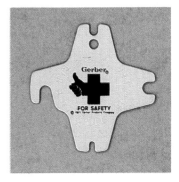

(Plate 54)

Plate 55 Gerber Corp. ID Items

Note pads, playing cards and letter opener all have Gerber and the Baby logo on each piece. **1990's**

Photo from Group II Communications.

Plate 56 Gerber Corp. ID Items

Twenty wooden match boxes with complete **assortment of corporate logos** embossed on metal covers and fit into a clear plastic container. The logos are: Gerber Babywear™, Gerber® with the Baby face, Buster Brown, Nodaway, Nursery™ Orginals, Gerber Life Insurance with the Baby face, Gerber® Children's centers, and KENT Inc. **1985**.

From the Shirley Brooks collection.

Plate 57 Gerber Corp. ID Items

Brass Coasters with leather pad and a brass etched medallion of the Gerber Baby in the center of each coaster. Two coasters are cased in an oak holder. **1990's**.

From the Bob Johnston collection

Plate 58 Gerber Corp. ID Items
Footed covered glass candy jar with the Gerber Baby etched into the glass.

From the Kyle Converse collection

(Plate 57)

(Plate 58)

Plate 59 Gerber Corp. ID Items

Gerber Baby Ladies watch. Slash marks are used to indicate the hours around the outside of the face. Leather strap. **1970's**. *From the Shirley Brooks collection.*

Plate 60 Gerber Corp. ID Items
Book Matches with a picture of the Gerber Baby on each packet. **1970's**

(Plate 59)

(Plate 60)

Plate 61 Gerber Corp. ID Items

Money Clips with the company logo and baby head. Top Row: **Silver clip** with gold medallion, G and the Baby head; **Gold clip** with Baby head medallion and diamond; Bottom Row: **Swiss Army Knife** in blue with Gerber and Baby head in silver. **Silver clip** with Gerber and Baby head screened in blue, and

Gold clip with attached medallion with G. and Baby head in blue. **circa. 1980's and 1990's.**

From Kyle Converse, Bob Johnston, and Lois Witte collections.

(Plate 61)

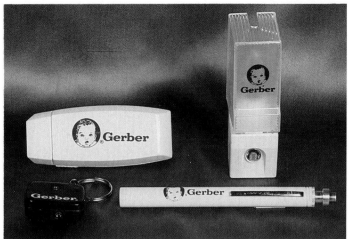

Plate 62 Gerber Corp. ID Items
Clip light attaches anywhere, has a powerful beam and includes batteries. **1986.** Gerber and the Gerber Baby face are printed on the light.**Dual purpose lighted key ring.1985.** Gerber is printed on the side of the case. **Night light (late 80's)** with Gerber and Baby head screened on surface. **Pen light, 1980** with Gerber and Baby head screened in blue.

(Plate 62)

From Kyle Converse and Bob Johnston collections.

Plate 63 Gerber Life Insurance Co.
Gerber Life Insurance Items: Golf Umbrella, Cap, Duffle Bag. *From the Ferol Dougan Borkowski collection.* **1990's** . **Calculator**.

From the Shirley Brooks collection **1980's.**

(Plate 63)

Plate 64 Jewelry, Pins
Lapel Pins: Gerber Graduates logo in 6 colors; **Lapel pin** with Gerber logo in gold on blue; **Gold lapel pin** with Gerber Baby face. **1990's**
Photo from Group II Communications.

(Plate 64)

Plate 65 Jewelry, Pins
Unisex analog **Quartz Watch** features Gerber Baby face. Gold plated with leather band. **1990's**

Photo from Group II Communications

(Plate 65)

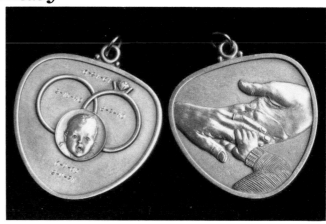

Plate 66 Jewelry, Pins
Solid Pewter Pendant designed for National Baby Week, **1979**, to honor children and their parents. Gerber contributed $.50 to CARE for each order. Front side: entwined rings with a third circle being the Gerber Baby head; Reverse side shows parents and baby hands together.

Photo from Gerber Archives

(Plate 66)

Plate 67 Jewelry, Pins
10 karat gold **Gerber Baby Stick Pin** in a lovely satin lined snap-close case. *1978.*
Photo from Gerber Archives

Plate 68 Jewelry, Pins
Spoon Ring made from an Oneida spoon. The Gerber Baby head is on top of the ring. The ring in the photo has four dates inscribed on the side of it. I do not know their significance.**1978.**
Photo from Gerber Archives

(Plate 68)   (Plate 67)

Plate 69 Jewelry, Pins
Top Row: **Charm bracele**t with Gerber baby face. **Bronze Plated Belt Buckle, with the Gerber Baby.** It was originally made to sell to employees and issued later as a **1976 premium** for $3.00 and 3 labels.   **Bronze charm** of Baby face was a service award, also found with precious stone chips designating years of service; dates from early years of the company.

(Plate 69)

Men's and Women's gold colored expandable Watch Bands with the Gerber Baby head at each end of the band. **1981.**
From the Kyle Converse and Bob Johnston collections.

Plate 70 Jewelry, Pins
4 Tie Tacks and Tie Clips featuring the Gerber Baby,Circa**70's and 80's** and a **Gerber 3rd Foods tie tack,1980's. Congratulations card with #1 tie tack, 1988.** *From the collections of Kyle Converse, Bob Johnston, Matt Okkema and Bob Robart.*

136

(Plate 70)

Plate 71 Jewelry, Pins

An Assortment of Gerber Baby Lapel Buttons. "I Have Visited the Gerber® Baby" lapel button was given to people who toured the plant beginning in **1941**. It was not issued during the war years as metal could not be secured. Prewar button measured 3 1/4' in diameter, the post war button was 1 3/8" dia.. **Gerber Baby® Lapel Pin** with a dark blue background. 2 1/2" in diameter. **Gerber Baby Lapel Pin**, outlined in blue on white background with blue border. 2 1/4" . **Gerber Graduates pin**, **Gerber Super Service Pin**, and a **VP Identification Pin**. **Gerber Baby Lapel Pin** with a dark blue background. 2 1/2" in diameter. **Gerber Baby Lapel Pin** .1 3/8". Under the picture are the words "Gerber's 25th Anniversary / 1928 -1958" "25". **Gerber Baby Lapel Pin , 3/4", with flag** which reads "Old Fashion Days / Fremont, Michigan". **1960's**

From the collections of Kyle Converse, Bob Johnston, and Bob Robart.

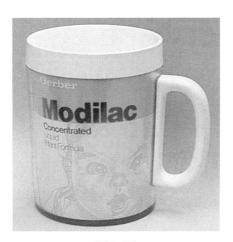

(Plate 72)

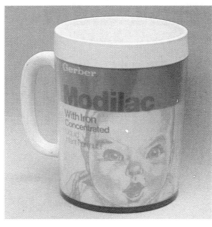

(Plate 73)

Plate 72 Mugs, Drinking Glasses

Plastic Mug with Modilac advertising between layers of plastic. One side is blue and the other side is orange. The Gerber Baby face is imprinted in the paper. **1960-70**.

Plate 73 Mugs, Drinking Glasses

Orange side of Modilac mug in Plate 72

(Plate 74)

Plate 74 Mugs, Drinking Glasses

Travel Mug with lid and special base which can be applied to dashboard, with Gerber Baby face in blue. **Can Cooler** features Gerber Baby face logo. **1990's.**
Photo from Group II Communications.

(Plate 75)

Plate 75 Mugs, Drinking Glasses

Insulated White Mug with Gerber and the Baby head in blue. **1988**

Plate 76 Mugs, Drinking Glasses
Ceramic Coffee mug with printed picture of the Gerber Baby® and a baby bottle, along with the words "Gerber baby formula / with iron / for baby's first year. " **1980's**

(Plate 76)

Plate 77 Baby Care/Wear
Reverse side of mug in plate 76 says "Congratulations for a successful First Year."

(Plate 77)

Plate 78 Mugs, Drinking Glasses
White mug with Gerber Baby face and "Safety and Quality / An Unbeatable Team / Fremont Plant / **1987**", screened on both sides.

(Plate 78)

Plate 79 Mugs, Drinking Glasses
Two ceramic mugs with Gerber and the Baby face on each. Mugs from **the 1980's.**

(Plate 79)

Plate 80 Mugs, Drinking Glasses
The reverse sides of the mugs in plate 79. The mug on the left is screened with a crown and the words" Let Safety Rule". and the mug on the right is screened with a red heart and says Safety / is the/ Heart / of/ success".

(Plate 80)

138

Plate 81   Mugs, Drinking Glasses

"I'm a Gerber BAD Guy" mug . Buck-A-Day (BAD) was the theme of a month long program at Moyer designed to actively involve all employees in helping to reduce costs while improving productivity. **1984.**

(Plate 81)

(Plate 82)

Plate 82 Mugs, Drinking Glasses

White ceramic mug with Gerber baby head and "Medical Services" screened on the side. The mug on the right is a **Stoneware coffee mug**, blue and white, **1988.** "Gerber" screened on side.

From the Bob Johnston collection

(Plate 83)

Plate 83 Mugs, Drinking Glasses

Ceramic Mugs left to right. **Modilac Mug**, blue on one side and green on the other. The words 'Concentrated/ Modilac/ Liquid Infant Formula' Gerber and Baby face are also screened on the surface,**1970. Dark blue mug** "Dollars for Ideas TOP" with the Gerber Baby face in the light bulb.

White mug with Gerber and the Baby face screened on one side and Safety Comes/ in Cans , with three dancing cans, on the reverse side.

From the collections of Kyle Converse, Matt Okkema and Bob Robart.

(Plate 84)

084 Mugs, Drinking Glasses

Reverse side of mugs described in Plate 83.

Plate 85 Mugs, Drinking Glasses

Blue ceramic coffee mug with the Gerber Baby picture and the words "Gerber Visitors Center / Grand Opening / September 10, **1990**".

From the collection of Matt and Doris Okkema.

(Plate 85)

Plate 86 Mugs, Drinking Glasses
Wonder Mugs. Uniquely designed for stability with rubber base. **Grabber Mug, 1984.** Gerber and the Gerber Baby head are screened on the side of the mug on the left. The blue insulated mug has a sip top to keep the contents from spilling. "Gerber" in white.

(Plate 86)

Plate 87 Mugs, Drinking Glasses
Insulated hot or cold beverage container with lid. 1988.
"Gerber®" printed on cup.

Plate 88 Mugs, Drinking Glasses
Silver metal cup with penny size Gerber Baby head fastened to side. **1990.** "Shirley / Jefferson Cup / Williamsburg, Virginia."

From Bob Johnston collection.

(Plate 88)

(Plate 87)

Plate 089 Mugs, Drinking Glasses
Glass Beverage Tumblers. A dozen of these 13 ounce glasses sold for $5.50 in **1978**. The Gerber Baby head is screened in blue on each glass. **Glass tumbler** with "Gerber / Baby Foods" and the Gerber Baby picture screened in blue.

(Plate 89)

(Plate 90)

(Plate 91)

Plate 90 Mugs, Drinking Glasses
Mug, 5 1/2". A picture of the Gerber Baby is on one side. On the other is a dancing clock which says, "Safety Around the Clock". **1980's**

Plate 91 Mugs, Drinking Glasses
Reverse side of dancing clock mug in Plate 90.

(Plate 92)

Plate 92 Novelty Dolls
"I'm A Gerber™ Kid" 11 1/2" Rag Doll. This cute doll could be either a girl or boy doll. The styles of kids' clothes have not changed much between **1984** and today. Made by Atlanta Novelty, Inc. The date of issue of the rag dolls is stamped on the back of the head.

From the Ellen Cappadonia collection

(Plate 93)

Plate 93 Novelty Dolls
"I'm a Gerber Kid ™" doll from 1984. This poor little lass had her apron sewn on backwards and upside down.
From the Barbara Howard collection.

(Plate 94)

Plate 94 Novelty Dolls
"I'm A Gerber™ Kid" 11 1/2" Dolls. Dressed in either dresses or play cloths these cuties were available from **1981 to 1984**. Made by Atlanta Novelty, Inc..

Plate 95 Novelty Dolls
"I'm A Gerber™ Kid" 8' Vinyl Boy and Girl Squeaker Dolls. The printed message on the visor of the boy's hat can be seen in this view of the back of the dolls. Circa. **1985**

Plate 96 Novelty Dolls
" I'm A Gerber™ Kid" 8" Vinyl Girl and Boy. These adorable squeaker toys by Atlanta Novelty, Inc. were made in **1985**. This view shows the printed message on the apron of the girl doll.

(Plate 95)

(Plate 96)

Plate 97 Paper, Pictures, Postcards
Gift Wrap Set includes two sheets of paper with pictures of the Gerber Baby, Gerber Baby card (blank inside) and bow. 1990's

From Bob Robart collection.

(Plate 97)

(Plate 98)

Plate 98 Paper, Pictures, Postcards
Stock Holders Gift Order Forms. Until Gerber Products Company was sold to Sandoz of Switzerland in 1994, stock holders were able to buy gift items such as toys, baby food gift packs, layette items, etc. directly from the company using these forms. **Gerber Foods coupon,** $1.00 value. **Gerber postcards** dating from the **1930's** show how the Fremont physical plant expanded over the years.

From the Marian Hart and Bob Robart collections

(Plate 99)

Plate 99 Paper, Pictures, Postcards
A collection of Company Greeting Cards. The card second from the left in the back row was made for Hallmark's Ambassador line and sold through grocery stores in the early **1990's.** It contained a message and a $1.00 off coupon.The three cards in the front row are from the early **40's and 50's**. They were sent to employees by Dan Gerber.

From the collections of Matt Okkema and Bob Robart.

Plate 100 Paper, Pictures, Postcards
Postcards. All Fremont Canning Company and Gerber Products Company postcards are collectible.

(Plate 100)

Plate 101 Paper, Pictures, Postcards
Gerber Baby® Picture.   The **1928** drawing by Dorothy Hope Smith of baby Ann Turner (Cook) became the the registered trade mark symbol of the Gerber Products Company. A copy of the 7 7/8" x 10" print is still available from Gerber Products Company. The original is locked in the company safe. This copy was signed by Ann Turner Cook when she visited Fremont to help celebrate the 50th anniversary of the company in **1978.**

From the Lois Witte collection

(Plate 101)

Plate 102 Paper, Pictures, Postcards
Picture. A free picture of a little girl sitting in an oversized wicker chair, dressed in a play suit and sun bonnet, while playing with a ball of yarn, was available from the company in **1961.** The ad appeared in the *Family Circle* magazine. See ad in Magazine Ad section of this book.

(Plate 102)

(Plate 103)

Plate 103 Paper, Pictures, Postcards
Picture. A picture of "the little charmer", was offered from **1963-1965**. The picture was part of an ad which often appeared in *Family Circle* magazine during this period. It was considered the most popular ad ever published by the company.
Picture from the Matt and Doris Okkema collection.

(Plate 104)

Plate 104 Paper, Pictures, Postcards
The **flip calendar** on the right features a different baby for each month of the year. Gerber and the Baby face appear on the border, **1990's**. **Gerber Baby Calendar** for **1989**. Imprinted: *"Gerber" / Babies are our business... and have been for over 60 years.*

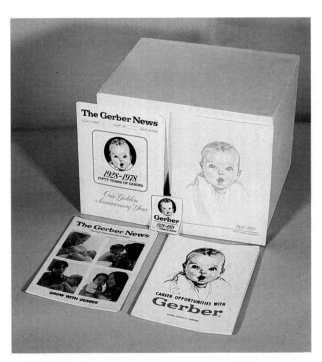
(Plate 105)

Plate 105 Paper, Pictures, Postcards
Gerber News Annual Stock Holders Report, Gerber News Golden Anniversary Issue,1978 Gerber Career Opportunities. *From the Barbara Maxson collection.*

Gerber Family News Release Folder.
From the Kyle Converse collection.

(Plate 106)

Plate 106 Pens, Pencils, Desk Items
Bic Pens with special message, "Call 1-800-4-GERBER for answers to questions on feeding and caring for your baby". **Highlighter /Pen** also features the special message. **Pencils**, with Gerber and the special message. **1990's**.
Photo from Group II Communications

Plate 107 Pens, Pencils, Desk Items
Baby bath thermometer from the 30's ;
Acrylic paper weight with timer and miniature
box of Gerber cereal encased inside. **1960. Pencil**
clips of the Baby face. **1930's**. Notice the two different styles.

From the Kyle Converse and Bob Johnston collections

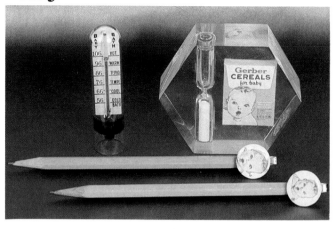

(Plate 107)

Plate 108 Pens, Pencils, Desk Items
A collection of **writing instruments** with the
company name and logo. Circa. **1980's and 1990's.**

From the Kyle Converse and Bob Johnston collections.

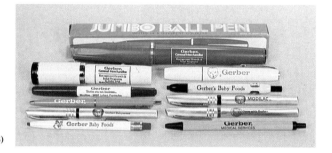

(Plate 108)

Plate 109 Pens, Pencils, Desk Items
Memo books in black leather.
Cross, chrome ball point and felt
tip pen set with raised baby head.
1988. Wood grained paper dispenser with Gerber and Baby head in
black, **1989. Letter opener** in case
which reads, *"Babies are our business...our only business.".* **(1970)**
Leather record / notebooks.

From the Shirley Brooks and Bob Johnston collections.

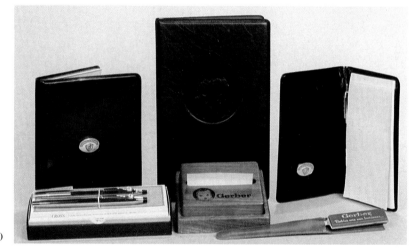

(Plate 109)

Plate 110 Pens, Pencils, Desk Items
13 inch Metal Ruler, "Gerber Baby Food"
consistent advertising in Family Weekly and
Suburbia Today assures an extra measure of
sales success" (**1960**). **12" Metal Ruler,** "Gerber
Baby Foods Consistently Advertises in Suburbia
Today." **1959**. 2 inputs
The **folding ruler** says "Gerber Employees
Fremont Federal Credit Union, **1970's**." The **6"**
plastic ruler says "Gerber's Baby Foods" . The
reverse side lists the Gerber® food line of products.**1950's**

From the Bob Johnston and Bob Robart collections.

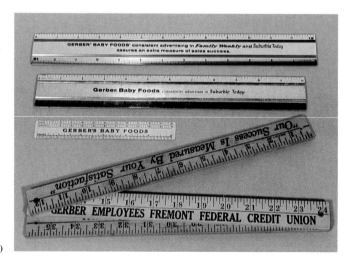

(Plate 110)

146

(Plate 111)

Plate 111 Pens, Pencils, Desk Items
An **assortment of desk items** featuring the name Gerber and the Baby head. Back row. **Digital clock card holder,1985; Paper clip dispenser, 1978; Wood grain desk organizer, 1989; Digital clock card holder,1989; Ball pen holder, 1972.**

Card holder, 1985; A Gold Metal Card Carrier which reads, "Gerber General Merchandising / First Million Dollar Sales Day/ June 28, **1985."**

From the Bob Johnston collection.

(Plate 112)

Plate 112 Production and Sales

Assortment of **paper items.** Back Row: **The Gerber News,** started as a newsletter for brokers and salesmen in **1931**. It became a tabloid newspaper, Vol. 1 No.1, on June 5, **1935**. It was called the Fremont Gerber News for the Fremont Canning Co. The word Fremont was dropped and it became a Company newspaper for all employees. **1961 Ambassador Program** for Salesmen **folder** which included **coupons** and a **tie tack;** Salesmen manuals : **Drivers Manual, Gerber Travel Guide.**

From the Bob Johnston Collection

(Plate 113)

Plate 113 Production and Sales Salesmen Directories and Calculators from the early **1990's.**

From the Bob Johnston collection.

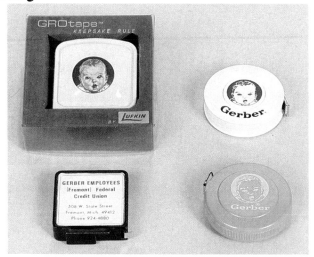

(Plate 114)

Plate 114 Production and Sales
Tape Measures. Top row: **Grotape** by Lufkin, **1969**; tape in **round white case** with Gerber and baby face. Bottom Row: **Fremont Federal Credit Union** tape for the Gerber Employees; a **tape cased in blue** with Gerber and baby head screened in white.

(Plate 115)

Plate 115 Production and Sales
Two color **tape measure**. Red underside, cream colored top with Gerber and baby head screened on top.

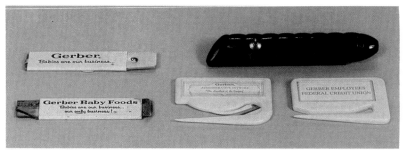

(Plate 116)

Plate 116 Production and Sales
Cafeteria tray, 1950's, and production line **worker's cap**. The Gerber baby head and "Quality is My Job / Gerber" is screened on the front of the cap. **1940's**

From the Bob Robart collection.

Plate 117 Production and Sales
Box Top Cutters: "Gerber Baby Foods / Babies are our business..../ our only business.!" Circa. **40's** "Gerber" / Babies are our business... Circa. **60's** **Paper Cutters:** 'Gerber Employees Federal Credit Union', and 'Administrative network'

Scrappers Knife. "Gerber / Babies are our business...our only business.", **1940's.**

From the Bob Johnston and Bob Robart collections.

(Plate 117)

148

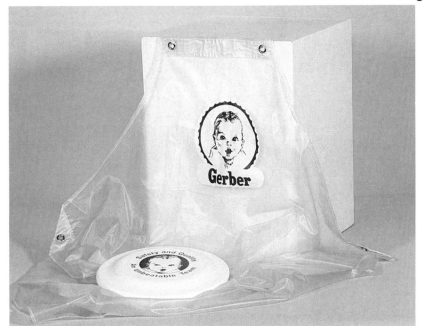

(Plate 118)

Plate 118 Production and Sales
Plastic Apron with the Baby Face.
(30's and 40's) The apron is full adult
size and was worn by the workers on
the line. **Frisbee** with Baby Face and
the words "Safety and Quality / An
Unbeatable Team." **(Mid 80's)**

(Plate 119)

Plate 119 Special Events
Gerber Baby Head Patches: (Left to
right) **Paper stick-on decal,** 2 1/2'
dia.**1970's**; '**Fifty Years of Caring, cloth
patch, 1978**; Gerber Baby® head cloth **sensitive patches. 1981**, $.60.
From Bob Johnston collection.

(Plate 120)

**Plate 120
Special Events**
**Q u a r t
Pitcher** with
etched picture of
the Gerber Baby
and "June 2,
1990 / Gerber /
Golf Open".
**"1989 Gerber /
Golf Open" hi
ball glass** with
etched picture of the Gerber Baby; **Glass tumbler** with
"Gerber" and the Gerber Baby picture etched in the glass.

Plate 121 Special Events
"Gerber 50th Anniversary Special" Plastic Baby Bottle
with $.35 off Gerber coupon and silver baby spoon inside. The
stainless steel spoon is marked on the underside "Gerber 50
Years of Caring 1928-**1978**". A **food bottle** from **1958** embossed
"25th Anniversary / Gerber" with the Gerber Baby head. The
back is embossed: "Gerber Plant Asheville, N.C. / 1958".

From the Bob Johnston collection.

(Plate 121)

Plate 122 Special Events
Six pack cooler. Made of molded plastic. It is blue with a white lid and handles "**1991** / Gerber® / Open".

(Plate 122)

Plate 123 Special Events
Styrofoam   Can Holder with a picture of the Gerber Baby and "Gerber / **1982** Open" printed in blue.

(Plate 123)

Plate 124 Special Events
Crystal Bell sent to executive's wives in appreciation for their support. The Gerber Baby face is etched in a 7/8" circle. A crystal bead hangs from a gold chain. Late **1980's.**

From the Matt and Doris Okkema collection.

(Plate 124)

Plate 125 Special Events
A tote bag screened "The Stork Club" with the Stork Club logo on one side and "Gerber®" with the Gerber baby head screened on the other, was a gift to the honored guests attending the 50th Anniversary of Gerber Products Company celebration at the Stork Club in New York. **1978**. Dark blue with white print. *From Matt and Doris Okkema collection.*

Plate 126 Special Events
An **invitation to attend an Open House** celebration at the Stork Club in New York City in honor of the 50th Anniversary of Gerber Products Company was given to a select list of honored guests. **1978**. *From the Matt and Doris Okkema collection.*

(Plate 125)

(Plate 126)

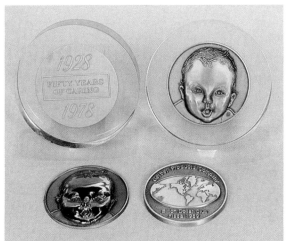

Plate 127 Special Events
Paper weights: Bronze coin encased in plastic, Coin reads "1928 / 50 Years of Caring / **1978**". Face of coin is the Gerber Baby head. Overall size, 3 3/4" dia. by 7/8' thick. Bottom Row: Same **bronze coin** as above but highly polished. **Bronze weight** with map,which reads 'Gerber Products Company / Billion Dollar Club / Fiscal **1989**.' *From Shirley Brooks, Kyle Converse and Bob Johnston collections.*

(Plate 127)

Plate 128 Special Events
Plastic Tote bag, white printed in blue. The Gerber Baby head and the words "Gerber / 1928-**1978** / Fifty Years of Caring".

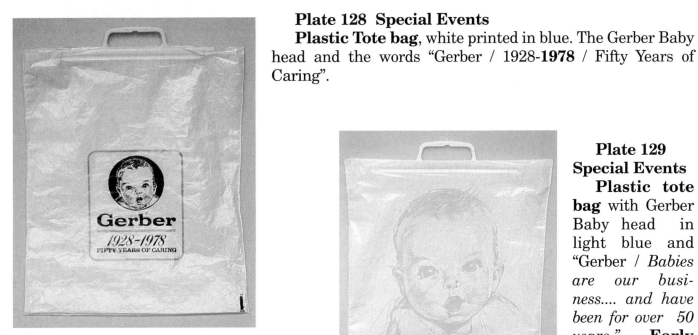

(Plate 128)

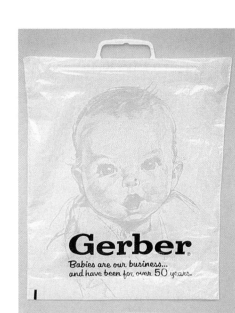

Plate 129 Special Events
Plastic tote bag with Gerber Baby head in light blue and "Gerber / *Babies are our business.... and have been for over 50 years.*" **Early 1980's.**

(Plate 129)

Plate 130 Special Events
Plastic tote bag with Gerber Baby head in light blue and "Gerber / *Babies are our business.... and have been for over 60 years.*" **Late 1980's.**

(Plate 130)

Plate 131 Special Events

Plastic tote bag with Gerber Baby head in dark blue and "Gerber / *Babies are our business.... and have been for over 60 years.*" Early **1990's**

(Plate 131)

Plate 132 Special Events 12" tray made to commemorate the 50th anniversary of the Gerber Products Company. It has a picture of the Gerber Baby head and the words "Gerber®

(Plate 132)

Baby Food / 1928-1978 / Fifty Years of Caring." Circa. **1978**

Plate 133 Sports and Leisure

Flying Disc, white with Gerber Baby in blue. **1990's**

Photo from Group II Communications

(Plate 133)

Plate 134 Sports and Leisure

Frisbee with large picture of the Gerber Baby .The words, "Safety Comes in Cans", above the picture, and "I Can, You Can, We Can" below the picture. Blue print on white plastic. Circa. **1980's**

(Plate 134)

Plate 135 Sports and Leisure
Sports Pouch, black nylon with "Gerber" in white.**1990's**

Photo from Group II Communications.

(Plate 135)

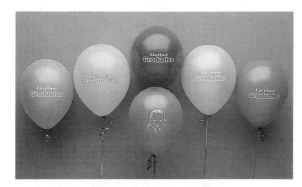

Plate 136 Sports and Leisure
Gerber Graduate balloons and **Gerber Baby head balloons. 1990's**.

Photo from Group II Communications

(Plate 136)

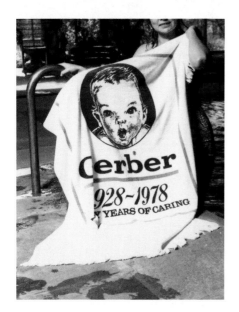

Plate 137 Sports and Leisure
Beach Towel, white velour with fringed edges. "Gerber / 1928-**1978** / 50 Years of Caring" and the Gerber Baby head are screened on the towel.

Photo from Gerber Archives

(Plate 137)

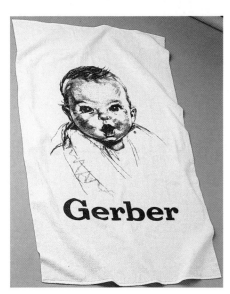

Plate 138 Sports and Leisure
Beach Towel, white velour. 35" x 62". **1988**. The name "Gerber" and the Gerber Baby face are on the front of the towel.

From the Matt and Doris Okkema collection.

(Plate 138)

153

Plate 139 Sports and Leisure
Rayon Canvas **Windjammer Duffel Bag** with waterproof interior. **1983**. Gerber® and the Gerber Baby face are printed on the front of the bag.

(Plate 139)

Plate 140 Sports and Leisure Tote bag.
Blue nylon, 14" x 11" x 51/2" , features Gerber Baby face on one side and Gerber logo on the opposite side. **1990's**

Photo from Group II Communications.

(Plate 140)

Plate 141 Sports and Leisure
Plastic **stadium cushion** with a picture of the Gerber Baby and the name "Gerber" in blue on white. Circa. **1980's**

From the Matt and Doris Okkema Collection

(Plate 141)

Plate 142 Sports and Leisure
Leather **Golf Glove** with Gerber baby screened on top side.1980's **Greenskeeper.** Slim pocket size made by Zippo. Ideal for repairing ball marks, cleaning spikes on shoes and marking balls on putting surface. **1983**, "Gerber®" and the Gerber Baby head are on the case.

Golf Balls, three in a package with the picture of the Gerber Baby and "Gerber". **1978**, $11.50 per dozen. **Golf Tees** (4) in white plastic belt holder. Imprinted "Gerber® / *Babies are our business...* / Modilac- MBF Infant Formulas / Baby Foods". **1970**.

From the Bob Johnston collection.

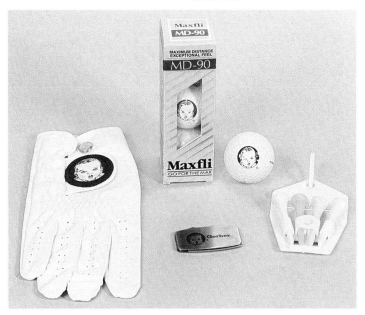

(Plate 142)

Plate 143 Sports and Leisure
Double deck sets of Gerber red and blue **playing cards** with the Gerber baby head. They came in either a plastic case or cardboard case. **1978**. Double Deck of **Playing Cards** (**green and white**) in a box. On each card is a picture of the Gerber baby and the words, "Gerber Baby Formula / Modilac". **1970**. Single Deck, dark blue with logo.

From Bob Johnston and Bob Robart collections.

(Plate 143)

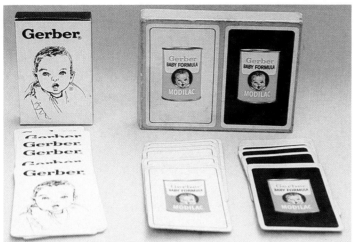

(Plate 144)

Plate 144 Sports and Leisure

Single decks of **Playing cards, white with Gerber Baby face in blue**, packaged two to a set. Double Deck of **Playing Cards (blue and white)** in a box. A picture of the Gerber Baby and the words, "Gerber Baby Formula / Modilac" are on each card. **1970.**

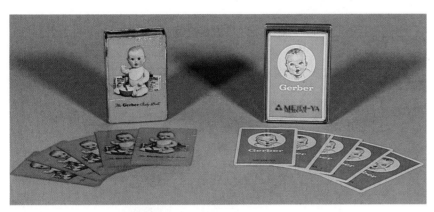

(Plate 145)

Plate 145 Sports and Leisure

Single deck of **Playing Cards** with the Gerber Baby face made for the Japanese market. **1970's**. *From the Shirley Brooks collection.* Single Deck of **Playing Cards** with a picture of the first real **Gerber baby doll made by Sun Rubber Co. in 1955.** *From the Barbara Maxson collection.*

Plate 146 Sports and Leisure

Gerber Spalding Championship **Tennis Balls**, three in a can. **1978.** Each ball is printed with "Gerber®" and the Gerber Baby head.

Photo from Gerber Archives

147 Sports and Leisure

Single Yellow **Tennis Ball. 1978.**

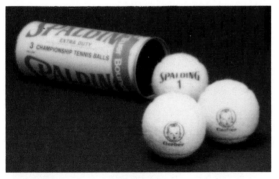

(Plate 146)

(Plate 147)

Plate 148 Sports and Leisure

White **Sports Hat** with a dark blue band and white Gerber logo. **1978.**

Photo from Gerber Archives

(Plate 148)

(Plate 149)

Plate 149 Sports and Leisure

Gerber **Running Shorts.** They are white with blue piping and a picture of the Gerber baby. **1978.**

Photo from Gerber Archives.

Plate 150 Time and Temperature Food Timer. Printed on the top: Safety / Gerber® / Takes Time. **1970's.**

(Plate 150)

Plate 151 Time and Temperature Outdoor thermometer, 14" x 5 3/4". Gerber and Baby head are featured at the top, *Babies are our business... and have been for over 50 years.* is printed at the bottom end of the thermometer. **1980.** *From Lois Witte collection.*

(Plate 151)

Plate 152 Time and Temperature Travel Alarm Clock, "Gerber" and Baby logo screened on base; **Wall Clock 12" dia**, "Gerber" and Baby head on face; **Desk Clock** Gerber Baby face screened in black. **1990's** *Photo from Group II Communications.*

(Plate 152)

Plate 153 Time and Temperature Wood Framed Clock, hexagon shape, 11 1/2" diameter overall, with a red sweep second hand. The 8 1/2" diameter face has a printed picture of the Gerber baby and the word GERBER®. Circa. **1970's**

Plate 154 Toys Gerber Lacing Shoe. The shoe does not bear the Gerber name or logo. However, the box is attractively decorated with "Gerber" and the Baby face. Molded by Arrow Molded Products Company, **1969.**

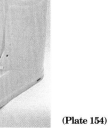

(Plate 153)

(Plate 154)

(Plate 155)

Plate 155 Toys
Gerber Baby Swiss Bells. A set of five colorful musical bells made of soft polyethylene, permanently decorated with the Gerber Baby face on each bell. They are attached to a vinyl band which is adjustable to fit a crib or playpen. By Arrow Molded Products. Circa. **1969.**

From the Sue Burness collection.

(Plate 156)

Plate 156 Toys
Talk-Back Phone designed with a hollow receiver so child can hear his own voice. It has a bright lithographed dial with Gerber Baby head in the center. By Arrow Molded Products. Circa. **1969.**

(Plate 157)

Plate 157 Toys
Gerber Jingle Blox. 1950's. These blocks are not marked with the Gerber logo. However, the box is attractively decorated with the Baby face in the letter G, and "Gerber" in white on blue.

From the Kyle Converse collection.

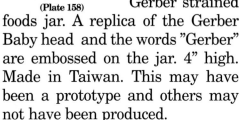

(Plate 158)

Plate 158 Toys
Squeaky Toy in the shape of a Gerber strained foods jar. A replica of the Gerber Baby head and the words "Gerber" are embossed on the jar. 4" high. Made in Taiwan. This may have been a prototype and others may not have been produced.

Plate 159 Toys
20" **Teddy Bears** made by Atlanta Novelty in **1978**. Their tags say 'Gerber/Tender/Loving/Care/Bear.'

From the Robert Robart collection.

(Plate 159)

Plate 160 Toys Stuffed Rabbit, made by Atlanta Novelty, a Subsidiary of Gerber Products Co. 13". Tag reads "Gerber® / Precious Plush". **1970's**.

(Plate 160)

(Plate 161)

Plate 161 Toys

Teddy Bear, 22" long. Made by Atlanta Novelty Inc. The Gerber / Care / Bear tag is missing but the cloth tag identifies it as an Atlanta Novelty toy. **1979-1985**. **"I'm a Gerber Baby Bib"** is made of terry cloth with a plastic backing. Circa. **1995**.

(Plate 162)

Plate 162 Toys

Small 6" **Stuffed Animals.** Available as a dog, cat, elephant, or bear, in a variety of colors. Made by Atlanta Novelty, Inc. a Subsidiary of Gerber Products Co. These toys were packed with 12" dolls. See Atlanta Novelty in the doll section of this book. Circa. **1979-1985**.

Plate 163 Toys

Teddy Bear Rattle. The tie on bib says "Peep", the cloth tag identifies it as Gerber Products Co. 6" tall. **1970's**

(Plate 163)

Plate 164 Toys

Carrying Case of Miniature Gerber Baby® Lotion Bottles and Cereal Boxes. This case was included as part of a set for the **1981** 12" Drink and Wet Doll by Atlanta Novelty, Inc.

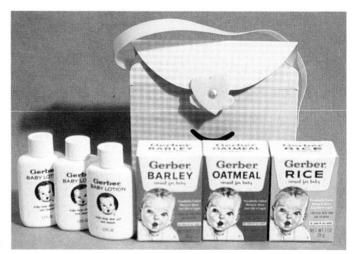

(Plate 164)

(Plate 165)

Plate 165 Toys
Gerber® Baby Blankie Bear which is sewn to its blanket is also a puppet. A rattle is built into the left paw and a squeaker into the right. Comes in pink or blue. *By Toy Biz*, Inc. **1994.**

(Plate 166)

Plate 166 Toys
Gerber® Baby Activity Mirror. While baby is looking at himself in the mirror pop-up talking friends appear on the screen. *By Toy Biz, Inc.* **1994**

(Plate 167)

Plate 167 Toys
Gerber Soft Touch Story Book presents words and sound effects of eight transportation vehicles complete with colorful graphics on 4 soft, durable fun filled pages. Requires 3"AAA" batteries. *By Toy Biz Inc.* **1994.**

Plate 168 Toys
Gerber® The Magic Message Phone records and plays 4 family messages. It has an auto ring back and busy signal, a colorful roller spinner and an easy grip handle. Requires 4 "AA" batteries. By Toy Biz, Inc. **1994.**
Photo by Toy Biz, Inc.

(Plate 168)

Plate 169 Toys

Gerber® Musical Dreamer Activity Screen is a high tech windup music box in which 8 pictures come alive. On the case are 5 classic busy activities. By Toy Biz, Inc. **1994**.

Photo from Toy Biz, Inc.

Plate 170 Toys (below)

Gerber® Baby Activity Computer has computer keys with electronic sounds and music, working mouse and track ball, 15 flash card activities and on board storage. Requires 4 "AA" batteries. By Toy Biz, Inc. **1994.**

Photo from Toy Biz, Inc.

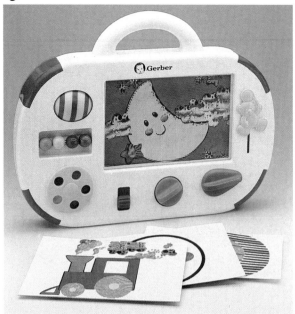

(Plate 169)

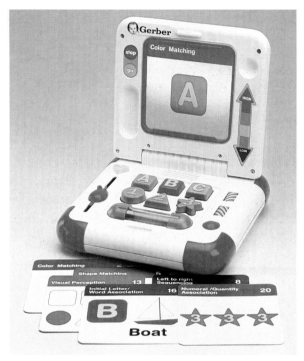

(Plate 170)

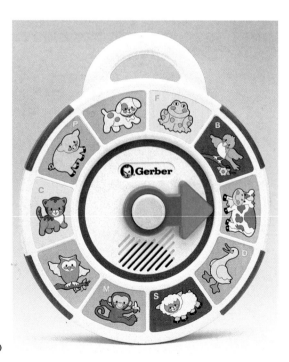

Plate 171 Toys

Gerber® 1,2,3 Discover! 3 levels of learning about animals include (1) animal sounds, (2) animals sounds and identification , and (3) sound, identification and initial alphabet letter. Requires 4 "AA" batteries. By Toy Biz, Inc. **1994**.

Photo from Toy Biz, Inc.

(Plate 171)

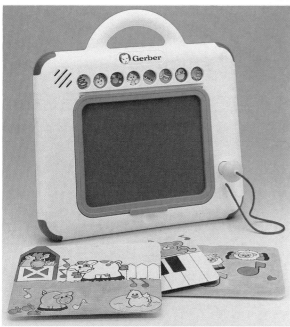

Plate 172 Toys
Gerber® Magic Musical Doodler, by Toy Biz, Inc. is made of high impact plastic. Create fun sounds and musical tunes as you doodle. The erasable magic slate eliminates the need for paper. Automatic shut off. Requires 4 "AA" batteries. **1995**.

Photo by Toy Biz, Inc.

(Plate 172)

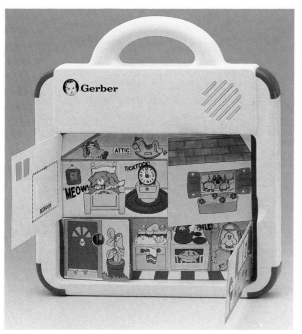

Plate 173 Toys
Gerber® Electronic Discovery Book contains 3 levels of learning about 8 animals and object identification of objects around the house. (1) Sound ID, (2) Name ID, (3) Sounds and Names combine in a short phrase. Requires 4 "AA" batteries. By Toy Biz, Inc. **1995**.

Photo by Toy Biz,Inc.

(Plate 173)

Plate 174 Trucks ans Trains
Gerber Semi Truck, with original box, designed in blue and white with the name of the company, pictures of animals, Gerber Baby head and the words "Baby Foods". 9 1/2" long. In the early years the double tandem trucks were used to transport baby food. Winross Mfg. **1978.**

From the Kyle Converse collection.

(Plate 174)

Plate 175 Toys
GMC "18 Wheeler" Nylint, No. 911 Z. 21 1/2" long. All steel construction with plastic roll-up back gate. A decal with "Gerber" along with the Gerber slogan and symbol are applied to the sides of the cab and the sides and front of the trailer. **1979.**

(Plate 175)

Plate 176 Trucks and Trains
Gerber® Box Car, HO Gauge. 5 3/4" long. Blue. Made by Bachmann in **1978** . The rail road car is an exact replica of the box cars used to ship the first train load of baby food to the southern states—Atlanta Ga. specifically, in the 30's.

(Plate 176)

Plate 177 Trucks and Trains
Gerber® Box Car, HO Gauge. 5 3/4" long. Pink. Made in China by Tyco. This box car is a reproduction of the blue box car made by Bachmann.

(Plate 177)

Plate 178 Trucks and Trains
Gerber® Baby Food Reefer, O gauge by Lionel, Number 6-9877. 11 1/2'" long. Blue with a picture of the Gerber baby and the words "Gerber ® / *Babies are our business...*" **1979.**

(Plate 178)

Plate 179 Trucks and Trains
Gerber Baby Food Reefer No. 87104 by Lionel. Large scale measures 5 1/2' high by 14 1/2' long. In green. **1990.**

(Plate 179)

Plate 180 Visitor Center, Guest House
Gift Box with Handle (3 1/2" x 2 1/4" x 7 1/4") . Printed on the cardboard box is, "Compliments of Gerber®" with the Gerber Baby head. A 5 1/2" Oneida Gerber baby spoon is attached to the outside of the box. 3 Gerber baby tumblers are inside. **Circa. 1990**

(Plate 180)

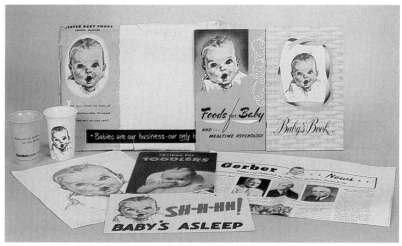

Plate 181 Visitor Center, Guest House

The **Visitor's Center Packet** contained six items in the **50's**: **Baby's Asleep sign**, a **picture** of the Gerber Baby, **3 booklets**, and a silk screened **plastic tumbler** with a picture of the Gerber Baby on one side and the words *"Babies are our business...our only business* on the other. *Babies' Book* was first printed in the early 30's. *Foods for Baby* and *Mealtime Psychology* were printed in **1952**.

(Plate 181)

A **copy of Gerber News** is also pictured. The Gerber News, started as a newsletter for brokers and salesmen in 1931. It became a tabloid newspaper, Vol. 1 No.1, on June 5, 1935. It was called the Fremont Gerber News for the Fremont Canning Co. *From the Kyle Converse collection.*

Plate 182 Visitor Center, Guest House
Visitor's Center Folder. "Welcome to Gerber" with a picture of the Baby on the front of folder. Imprinted on the folder is a short history of Gerber Products Company and a listing of things to see. Inside the folder is a **picture of the Gerber Baby, 3 D glasses** and a **Facts Folder**.   Circa. **1990** The Baby picture in this plate was signed by Ann Turner Cook in 1978.

"Baby Takes" is an informative card about the 3D movie which was shown at the Visitor Center. Yellow flyer tells about the activities at the Visitor's Center.

From the Bob Johnston and Lois Witte collections.

(Plate 182)

Plate 183 Visitor Center, Guest House
"Welcome to the Gerber House" was a 5 page history of the Gerber family and Fremont. The **small glass** is marked 'Gerber Guest House'. The guest house which was available to out of town salesmen and other company personal for lodging while in Fremont, was closed December 31, **1994.**

From the Bob Johnson Collection

(Plate 183)

Addedum:

Plate 184-185
Mugs, Drinking Glasses - Pop Can Holder
With picture of Gerber Baby on one side and "Safety is just a Thought Away"

(Plate 184)

Plate 186 Toys - Toy Cans of Gerber Baby Juice
The cans are regular size, but the metal top has the word "toy" pressed into it.

(Plate 185)

(Plate 186)

Collectibles Identified But Not Found

Pocket calendar and ruler given to brokers and salesmen as a promotional item in **1934-35.**

Tool crib set. Each plant employee had his own set. When the employee had to barrow a company tool for a company job he left one of his metal tags until he returned the tool. **1947-1956.**

Paper hat worn by male employees or men taking tours as a sanitation guarantee. Circa: **1960-** . Gerber® and the Gerber baby head are printed on the paper.

Educator spoon and fork set. This set was initially available as a **premium** in **1938** without the trademarked handles. The Gerber® trademark first appeared on the handles in 1941. Available for 15 cents and 3 labels.

Gerber Products Co. button showing a box of cereal, one of strained oatmeal, and two jars from the junior line of foods. The button was a one time promotional item worn by salesmen in the early 1940's

Tongue depressor and light which was given to doctors in the late **1960's** as a medical marketing promotional instrument.

Cost and selling price indicator used by Fremont Canning Co. salesmen around **1934.** The indicator worked something like a slide rule. The salesman could set the mark at the approximate cost figure and reading from the lower index he could readily determine the percent of profit.

Gerber® Executive (nylon) Laundry Bag. 1988.

Canvas Apron in beige with pocket in 25" x 38" size. **1988.** The name Gerber and the Gerber baby face are on the front of the apron.

Rugby Style Shirt. The name Gerber® is on the pocket of the shirt. **1988.**

Blue Nylon Flight Bag, 11 1/2" x 13" x 5". Gerber® is printed on the front pocket. 1988.

120 pound PSI tire pressure gauge in plastic case. 1986. Gerber® on gauge and case.

Safety Light to carry in your automobile for those "hope not" emergencies, plugs into lighter socket. **1988.** Gerber® printed on light.

Rubberbody Flashlight with magnetic pedestal, batteries included. **1988.** Gerber® and the Gerber baby face are printed on the end of the flashlight.

Flannel Lined Award Jacket. Gerber® printer on pocket. Circa. **1988.**

P's Bar writing set includes yellow underliner, water based blue and red ball- point pens, oil based black ball- point pen and brown mechanical pencil in white or black case. **1988.** Gerber® printed on side of case.

3 in 1 Opener. 1988. Gerber® printed on side.

USA Factory in black or white. It is a scissors, hole punch, stapler, magnifier, tape dispenser, ruler, staple remover and more. **1988.** Gerber® printed on side of case

Easily inflatable Sleepy Eye neck pillow in gray with plastic carrying folder. **1988.** Gerber® printed on folder.

Aladdin plastic quart thermos with carrying strap in dark blue. **1988.** Gerber® printed on side of container.

2'x 3' **Calendar** for all 365 days in blue. **1988.** Matching **Address book** also available. Gerber® printed on front of each.

3" x 4 1/2" maroon **Memo pad. 1988.** Gerber® printed on front. :

Zippo Tape Measure has retractable white blade with inch and metric measure to 78 " (200 CM). **1984.** Gerber® and Gerber baby head are printed on the case.

Plastic Foldable Hanger with Brush. 1984. Gerber® and the Gerber baby head are printed on the hanger.

Zippo Pill Box. specially designed for durability and has a handy slide -out tray. **1984.** Gerber® and the Gerber baby head are printed on the case.

Desk Organizer with several departments. **1983.** Gerber® and the Gerber baby head are printed on the side of the case.

Luggage Tag Holder. Tough with a latigo leather strap and heavy chrome plated roller buckle. ID card furnished. **1983.** Gerber® and "Babies are our business..." are printed on the leather.

Notables. 900 sheets of 3 1/2" x 1/2" sheets of paper, **1983.** Gerber® and the Gerber baby head are printed on the sides of the stack.

Household Record File with 24 picture pockets complete with record cards. **1983.** Gerber® printed on the cover.

Ice scraper with a 25" long handle, with a brush on one end and a squeegee on the other. **1983.** Gerber® and the Gerber baby head are printed on the handle.

Extra large Windshield Washer. 1983. Gerber® and the Gerber baby head are printed on the handle.

Zippo Navy Colored Belt with Buckle. 1983. Gerber® and the Gerber baby head are printed on buckle.

Desk Pad. 17" x 22", 50 sheets. **1983.** Gerber® and the Gerber baby head are printed on each sheet.

Potholder, 8". **1983.** Gerber® and the Gerber baby head are printed on the holder.

Portable Brush. Case is high impact styrene plastic and the brushes are washable nylon. Carries flat. **1983.** Gerber® and "Babies are our business …" are on the case.

Dark Blue Nylon Windbreaker. It was unlined and had a draw string. **1978.** The Gerber Baby ® was printed on the jacket.

Gerber Logo Ties in two color patterns: dark blue with red Gerber logo and brown with light blue Gerber logo. **1978.**

Gerber Tie. 100 % polyester material in blue with white Gerber baby heads. **1982.**

100 % polyester blue cloth with white Gerber baby heads. 1982.

Sport type wrist watches. Men's and Women's watches were black faced with gold toned stretch bands and the raised Gerber baby head. **1982.**

Cricket Disposal lighter. 1978. Gerber logo on case.

12 Quart White Waste Basket. 1978. Gerber and Gerber baby head on basket.

Durable, three piece set of dark blue nylon luggage: Tote bag. . carry-on bag with hanger, travel kit. Gerber® imprinted on each piece. Circa. **1986**

Zippo Key Holder in blue with the Gerber baby head.**1986.**

Fizz Whiz Beverage Caps. 1986. Gerber ® printed on side of cap.

Mainliner Baby Kit. 1938. United Airlines placed a Kit at each landing field. It contained evaporated milk, graham crackers, zwieback, and an assortment of all 11 strained baby foods. Kits were imprinted, "This variety of Gerber's Baby Food has been approved by the Council on food and the AMA.

Blue Nylon Duffel Bag, 10" x 19", with sturdy cloth handles and adjustable shoulder straps. **1985.** The Gerber logo and the Gerber baby head, plus other company logos, are printed in white on the bag.

Blue cloth six pack insulated cooler with handles and zipper. **1985.** Gerber® and the baby head along with other companies' logos are printed on the pack.

Scraper mitten. 1985. Gerber® printed on the outside of the mitten.

Durable plastic lock with 30" metal cable, four number combination. **1985.** Gerber® and the baby head are printed on the lock.

All silk blue women's tie (square ends) with the Gerber Baby . It was 2" wide and came in a gift box. **1985.**

Blue nylon wrist-ankle wallet with digital quartz watch and velcro fastener. **1985.** Gerber® printed on band.

Two piece travel toothbrush that fits into plastic travel case, complete with miniature toothpaste. **1985.** Gerber® printed on the outside of the case

Miniature screwdriver set in durable plastic case. **1985.** Gerber ® printed on the outside of the case.

Miniature Rocking Chair hand made by Lloyd and Ruth Kirby from Gerber Orange juice cans. Available from designer. **1978.**

I will be searching for these items and others still to be indentified. If you have them or know of others, let me hear from you!

Part 3
Gerber Magazine Advertising from 1930 to 1981

Unseasoned
Strained
Ready-to-Serve

for baby

Gerber's Strained Vegetables are scientifically prepared for the daily vegetable supplement to baby's milk diet. No salt, sugar or seasoning of any kind is added to the choice, fresh vegetables used in preparing the Gerber Products. Each product is strained to the smooth, even texture prescribed by most doctors. Each product is specially cooked and is ready-to-serve when seasoned as your own individual feeding problem requires.

Convenience and Wholesomeness

To the mother confronted with the daily task of preparing baby's strained vegetables in the home, the scientifically prepared, tested and approved Gerber Products offer hours of freedom from tedious kitchen tasks. And the rich mineral salt values and Vitamin A, Vitamin B, and Vitamin C that are partially destroyed under ordinary methods of home preparation are conserved in the maximum degree for baby by the Gerber steam-pressure process. Each product is steam-pressure cooked—sealed and steam-sterilized. Your doctor will gladly explain why the Gerber Products are best for baby. Consult him for the personal counsel that will insure the most effective variety for your own baby.

Special Introductory Offer

Gerber's Strained Vegetables are available at many leading grocers throughout the United States. If your own grocer is not yet able to supply you, send us today the coupon below with $1.00 for our complete introductory assortment—or order such single products as you wish. Postage prepaid. *In Canada, Complete Assortment Only, $1.10—Canadian Currency or Money Order.*

Free samples on request to Physicians or Hospitals.

★ Gerber's
STRAINED VEGETABLES

SEND THE COUPON TODAY—A WEEK'S SUPPLY

Gerber Products Division, *Fremont Canning Co.*, Fremont, Mich.
$1.00 Complete   Dept. GH-11 — Enclosed find money or stamps
Assortment   for Assortment or for Gerber Products checked.

15c	15c	15c	15c	15c	15c	15c
Strained Vegetable Soup	Strained Spinach	Strained Carrots	Strained Prunes	Strained Peas	Strained Tomato	Strained Green Beans

Name...

Address..

City............................State..................

My grocer is..

March 1930 Good Housekeeping

1930 Ad from Good Housekeeping shows first can with tumbling blocks & offer of free samples.

169

Better Homes and Gardens Ad- Oct. 1931

Indexed as: Fremont Canning Co. (Gerber Products) Note: first strained foods label- 3 tumbling blocks

Do you know what to do with this problem?

COUNTLESS mothers are struggling with the problem of the child that "won't eat." Little babe—toddler—and even the older child present this difficult attitude—because it is so largely just *attitude*. The modern mother is interested not only in what to feed her baby or young child—but *how* to feed him.

Ask Your Doctor

Baby's doctor should be consulted on the question of *what* your own individual baby's diet should be. He will be glad to explain why vitamin and mineral salt conservation give the Gerber Products an important place in baby's diet. You will find your doctor interested, too, in the question of baby's attitude toward food.

Send for Free Booklet

Dr. Lillian B. Storms, Director of the Department of Education and Nutrition of the Gerber Products Division, has just completed a new booklet which should be welcomed by mothers in their study of the question of baby's mealtime psychology. In addition to its discussion of the preparation, general function and food values of the Gerber Products, Dr. Storms' booklet contains much that should be of interest to the thousands of mothers who are struggling—largely alone—with the problem of the child that won't eat. Fill in the coupon below, and we will gladly mail you a copy.

Strained Vegetable Soup Strained Carrots - Strained Prunes-Strained Spinach Strained Tomatoes Strained Peas - Strained Green Beans.

15c at grocers and druggists

Gerber's STRAINED VEGETABLES

Dr. Lillian B. Storms, Ph.D., Director, Dept. of Education and Nutrition, Gerber Products Div., Fremont Canning Co., Fremont, Mich.
Please send free copy of your booklet "Baby's Vegetables and Some Notes on Mealtime Psychology."

Name_____
Address_____ BH-5

Important to Mother and Baby

MORE than the saving of time and effort which they mean to you each day—these special features of Gerber preparation are important because they make Gerber's Strained Vegetables *better for baby*.

1. When you prepare baby's vegetables, do you use ordinary market produce which may be days—even weeks—old? The Gerber Products are cooked under laboratory conditions while they're still crisp and garden fresh.

2. When you cook vegetables at home, vitamins are destroyed by oxidation. In the Gerber scientific autoclaves maximum conservation of vitamins is effected.

3. The difficult straining process at home further destroys the vitamin values. Gerber Vegetables are forced through a monel metal strainer with oxygen excluded, and valuable vitamins conserved.

4. The Gerber monel metal strainer is five times as fine as the ordinary kitchen sieve. It removes indigestible fibre that has no food value for baby.

5. When the water in which a vegetable has been cooked at home is poured away, it carries with it valuable mineral salts. The Gerber cooking process, and the vacuum pans used for bringing the products to uniform consistency conserve all important mineral values.

After the Gerber Products have been strained and sealed in steam washed cans they are subjected to a temperature which is past the thermal death point of any harmful bacteria that might be present. This is the process which preserves the products indefinitely.

More than 84,000 physicians have examined the Gerber Products. Ask your doctor about them for your baby.

Free Booklet

Mail the coupon below for the Gerber booklet which describes the Gerber Products in detail and offers many helpful suggestions for training baby's mealtime habits.

Strained Tomatoes Beets - Peas - Carrots Vegetable Soup - Prunes Green Beans - Spinach

15¢ at grocers and druggists

Better Homes and Gardens Ad- Sept. 1932

Indexed as: Gerber Products Co.

Note change in name from 1931. Also note label change.

Gerber's STRAINED VEGETABLES

LILLIAN B. STORMS, PH. D., GERBER PRODUCTS COMPANY, FREMONT, MICHIGAN
Please send me free copy of your booklet "Baby's Vegetables and Some Notes on Mealtime Psychology."

Name.................................
Address.................... BH-7

To PUZZLED Fathers

of rather young children

*M*RS. DAN GERBER *with* PAULA GERBER *at the age of 5 months. Youngest of the three Gerber children, Paula began to eat Gerber's Strained Cereal at 3 months, and had her first Gerber's Strained Vegetables at 3¼ months.*

*I*F YOU'VE *had to exchange a charming wife for a tired little mother who spends endless hours in the kitchen dutifully scraping, stewing and straining vegetables for your small son or daughter — you'll be glad to read this story.*

Five years ago, Mr. Dan Gerber faced the same situation, and knowing a great deal about vegetables, he set out to solve this problem. The result was Gerber's Strained Vegetable Products—now widely prescribed by physicians—so helpful to mothers and children everywhere.

Of course, your baby can thrive without the Gerber Products. But we feel sure your wife will appreciate your interest in learning more about these foods. Ask your doctor! He will tell you why they save baby's mother hours of time and effort— and more important—why foods prepared the Gerber way are better, safer for baby.

Gerber's Strained Vegetables are not medicinal. They are simply fine, fresh vegetables—a strictly essential part of baby's diet—prepared in such a way that their minerals and natural food elements can be best utilized by small stomachs. We can prepare them better than can be done at home because—we raise our own vegetables, so there's no uncertainty about their crisp,

Ask Your Doctor

garden freshness—we have special straining and cooking equipment to effect maximum conservation of true flavor and natural food elements (vitamins and minerals). Strained, uniform, unseasoned—they are *always ready* to warm and use as the doctor directs.

BABY'S CEREAL

Gerber's Strained Cereal is an infant cereal—not an adaptation of a general purpose cereal. The combination of whole wheat, hulled oats and added wheat germ, long cooked in whole, fresh milk, produces an ideal blending of important food values—and a flavor so appealing that many babies who resist ordinary cereal, eat Gerber's Strained Cereal with relish.

The rich food values of the bran are first cooked into the cereal, after which the harsh bran hulls are strained out. Strained, thoroughly cooked, it's all ready to warm and use.

The Gerber Products enjoy the acceptance seal of the Committee on Foods of the American Medical Association which not only accepts the products themselves but the things we say about them.

Strained Tomatoes, Carrots, Vegetable Soup, Beets, Prunes, Spinach, Peas, Green Beans — 4½ oz. cans

Strained Cereal—10¼ oz. cans
15c at Grocers and Druggists

Helpful Booklet FREE — Send Coupon

Gerber's for baby

9 KINDS OF STRAINED FOODS

ACCEPTED AMERICAN MEDICAL ASSN. Committee on Foods

GERBER PRODUCTS CO., FREMONT, MICH.
(*In Canada*) FINE FOODS OF CANADA, LTD., Windsor, Ont.

Please send me free copy of your booklet, "Baby's Vegetables and Cereal; Some Notes on Mealtime Psychology." (Enclose ten cents if you would also like a picture of the original Gerber Baby drawing by Dorothy Hope Smith.)

Name ....

Address D-26

June 1933- This ad features Dan and Dorothy Gerber's third daughter, Paula. The coupon is for free copies of Baby's Vegetables, and Meal Time Psychology.

America's Best-Known Baby

So many mothers tell me how much they appreciate having foods of the same brand for baby at every age! I'm proud it's Gerber's. You see, all the many Gerber Baby Foods really grew out of this one mother's happy suggestion about raising special vegetables for babies. Even though it was my husband, Dan Gerber, who put the idea to work!

Mrs. Dan Gerber

Gerber's Cereal Food

In every way it's a special babies' cereal: Dietitians helped develop it. It's enriched in iron and Vitamin B_1, *very* important for your baby. It has real flavor and the consistency babies like. And it's pre-cooked and ready to serve! *Send for free sample!*

Women's Day, 1941

Premium Ad for first Gerber Baby Spoon.

Gerber's Strained Foods

The vegetables are home-grown from selected seed *specially for babies.* Then they're tenderly, thoroughly cooked without pouring off the mineral-laden juices! 15 varieties of Gerber's Strained Foods include 2 savory soups, 7 vegetables, 5 tasty desserts.

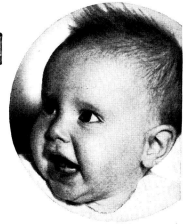

Gerber's Junior Foods

When your baby is ready for a coarser diet, we're ready with a whole line of Junior Foods. They're the same size and price as the Strained Foods. Just right for an average serving without leftovers. 9 delicious varieties including chopped vegetables.

For handsome International Silver plated baby spoon, send 10¢ plus 6 labels or box tops from Gerber's Baby Foods. Print your name and address carefully. Gerber's, Dept. 12, Fremont, Mich.

Gerber's
Baby Foods

"From a few weeks to a few years"

America's Best-Known Baby

Letters by the hundreds (yes, hundreds!) are coming in from mothers telling how excited they are about the new Gerber's Strained Oatmeal. Most babies apparently take to it with gusto -- a feature mothers seem to appreciate quite as much as the labor-saving angle. I must say this checks with my own experience with Dan, Jr., my youngest, whose picture you'll find at the bottom of the page. *Mrs Dan Gerber*

When babies can be choosers

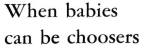

You and baby both will appreciate the luxury of choosing from three Gerber Cereals— all *dietitians'* cereals developed specially for babies . . . Gerber's Strained Oatmeal is that mealtime blessing—a babies' oatmeal you serve right from the box. Simply add milk or formula . . . Gerber's Cereal Food is a wheat-and-wheat-germ cereal of the same completely cooked, ready-to-serve type. Especially tasty . . . Gerber's Cooked-in-Milk Cereal adds extra calcium and phosphorus to the diet. This one comes in the handy-size strained food cans.

 Also on the Gerber menu: A complete array of strained foods featuring luscious *home-grown* vegetables. 2 soups, 8 vegetables, 6 desserts . . . 10 tasty Junior Foods (they're chopped) for senior babies. You'll find the same-size, same-price can both economical and handy.

Dan Gerber, Jr.

Free Samples

Gerber's, Dep't. 111, Fremont, Mich.

Please send me free samples of Gerber's Strained Oatmeal and Gerber's Cereal Food.

NAME . . . .

ADDRESS . . . .

CITY AND
STATE . . . .

Gerber's
Baby Foods

"From a few months to a few years"

Women's Day, 1941

This ad features Dan Gerber, Jr. The coupon is for free samples of <u>Gerber Strained Oatmeal and Gerber's Cereal</u> *food.*

See plate 23

Women's Day, Feb. 1945

This ad features Mrs. Dan Gerber in her column which preceeded "Bringing Up Baby". The coupon is for free cereal samples.

ONE
MOTHER
TO
ANOTHER

So much precious time is saved mothers by prepared baby foods. As a busy mother, that was the reason behind my suggestion to my husband, 16 years ago, that he pioneer in producing prepared baby foods.

Mrs. Dan Gerber

Mothers, you can buy a smile like this! ·

The smile of a happy, well-fed baby who *enjoys* his food! For that is one of the strong points of Gerber's Baby Foods—they taste *extra* good. Add to that their smooth, even texture, just right for easy digestion. Be sure to get Gerber's Baby Foods—cooked by steam to preserve precious minerals and vitamins to build healthy babies! *There are 15 Gerber's Strained Foods, also 8 kinds of Gerber's Chopped Foods for older babies.*

Oh, Hullo—have you heard, too?

About serving variety in cereals, I mean. Mummy serves Gerber's Cereal Food at one feeding, Gerber's Strained Oatmeal at the next. Because variety helps babies eat better. Both cereals are fortified with iron and Vitamin B_1. Both are pre-cooked —just add hot or cold milk or formula and serve.

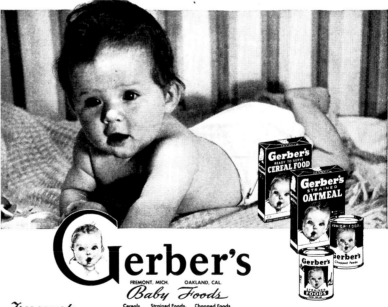

Gerber's
Baby Foods
FREMONT, MICH.   OAKLAND, CAL.
Cereals   Strained Foods.   Chopped Foods

Free sample

Address: Gerber Products Company, Dept. 12-5,   Fremont, Michigan

Please send me free samples of Gerber's Strained Oatmeal and Gerber's Cereal Food.

Name...

Address...City and State...

Some babies go for spoon-pounding in a big way... (that's just healthy self-expression).
Some fling empty dishes at the floor (just getting used to new equipment).

BUT more babies go for Gerber's than any other Baby Foods! So ask the doctor about starting your tot on good-tasting Gerber's Cereals— often the *very first* solid food after milk. When the time comes for Strained Foods—and later Junior Foods—continue with the baby favorites *more doctors approve*— Gerber's Fruits, Vegetables, Meat-combinations, Desserts!

ONE MOTHER TO ANOTHER

Many mothers write that Gerber's Junior Foods give baby variety with less leftovers. Why? Because of the same size container at this same low price as Gerber's Strained Foods.

Mrs Dan Gerber

For FREE SAMPLES of Gerber's 3 Cereals, write to Gerber's, Dept. W1-8, Fremont, Mich.

1948
This ad introduces the famous slogan "Babies are our business... our only Business".

Babies are our business... our only business!

Gerber's
BABY FOODS
FREMONT, MICH.   OAKLAND, CAL.
3 Cereals • 18 Strained Foods • 13 Junior Foods

175

APRIL 1949

Family Circle- 1949

The name of Mrs. Gerber's column has changed to "Mothers Club News"

He's happy we're minding our business!

You see, our business—our *only* business is making baby foods that baby enjoys.

No tricks, mind you! Only thing we do is make *True-Flavor* Foods that go over big with small folks coast-to-coast.

What makes Gerber's taste so good? Years and years of practice in turning out baby foods just right for tiny tots. Is your

small He or She enjoying the *natural goodness* of Gerber's? And that perfected texture?

Why do doctors approve Gerber's? Did you guess vitamins and minerals? Right! We've learned how to retain them to a high degree—in everything from Starting Cereals to Junior Meats.

Aren't you and baby glad we're busy minding our business!

Menu Planner For Mothers

Gerber's 45 True-Flavor Foods make it so easy to serve baby tempting, well-varied meals.

3 CEREALS
21 STRAINED FOODS
15 JUNIOR FOODS
3 STRAINED MEATS
3 JUNIOR MEATS

Gerber's
BABY FOODS
Fremont, Mich.

Babies are our business ... our only business!

Mothers Club News

Reported by

Mrs. Dan Gerber
(Mother of 5)

MEMBERSHIP REPORT: Every mother in America with a baby aged 1 day and up can belong! *No club dues—no initiation!* So why not have a lot of free fun swapping baby stories! You can collect a lot of helpful hints, too—via Mothers Club News!

LIGHT TOUCH. A small light attached to baby's crib won't keep him awake, will keep you from stumbling.

RAVE NOTICES on new meats. I can report to you that mothers from Maine to California are cheering the true-meat flavor of Gerber's Beef, Veal, Liver.

And what enthusiasm for the appetizing color and texture! Prepared from Armour quality cuts, Gerber's Meats for baby are ready to eat! No scraping!

ECONOMY NOTE: When baby graduates from Gerber's Strained Meats to Gerber's Junior (chopped) Meats, you pay the same modest price. What a saving compared to the cost of home-prepared meats.

≡FREE≡
≡FOOD≡

Send for samples of Gerber's 3 good-tasting Baby Cereals all with added iron, calcium and important vitamins. Write to Dept. 194-9, Fremont, Mich.

Accepted by the Council on Foods and Nutrition of the American Medical Assoc.

Bringing Up Baby

HINTS COLLECTED BY

Mrs Dan Gerber

(MOTHER OF 5)

Mrs. Gerber

If your pride and joy is old enough to hold up his head, he's ready for a little exercise. Grasp his (or her) hands and pull gently to sitting position. Three- or four-months' old babies chortle with glee over this kind of play.

* * *

Room service. Does your baby sleep in your room? It's wise to move him out before he is six months old. If, like so many young couples, you don't have an extra bedroom, a screen, homemade by papa, can give you and baby needed privacy.

* * *

First birthday. Now baby is probably ready to learn how to chew, so start serving Gerber's Junior Foods if you haven't done so. Menu for a Gerber-good birthday: Gerber's Junior Beef, green Spinach 'n golden Squash. And to make it an occasion baby won't forget, end up with Gerber's wonderful Orange Pudding!

The children's hour. The toys youngsters like best are the ones scaled to their size. A small woolly animal is much more dearly loved by a one-year-old than a large one.

* * *

Taking a hint. Some of our readers want to know if the hints in these columns come in book form. They haven't all been put between covers, but those mentioned above are from our "Baby's Book." A copy of this 32-page book of hints may be had for the asking. Just write me at Dept. 46-1, Fremont, Mich. In Canada, write Gerber-Ogilvie Baby Foods, Ltd., Niagara Falls, Canada.

This is one Peach that doesn't have to blush

RIGHT now millions of sweet-looking peaches (the tree-growing kind) are growing up in the warm sun getting ready for the big day when they are picked and processed for that sweet peach of *yours.*

So count on lots of sunny smiles at mealtime! For our peaches come from healthy trees and are selected especially for babies. Color-right, flavor-right, texture-right. Sweet 'n luscious, and just about the best Mother Nature can produce.

Note this for nutrition: Gerber's

Peaches help babies get the Vitamin **A** they need and are a good source of *iron.* That's why they are among the first fruits added to baby's diet. *All* Gerber's Fruits, Vegetables, Meats, Cereals and Desserts are flavor-true and true in nourishment, because we spend all our time making baby foods and nothing else.

Have you tried our Meats? They supply important body-building proteins which babies need in summer as well as in winter. Gerber's Strained and Junior Meats cost far less than meats cooked and scraped at home.

Babies are our business . . . our only business!

Gerber's
Baby Foods

Good Houskeeping- 1951

The beginning of Mrs. Gerber's famous "Bringing Up Baby" column. It will continue through the 50's and 60's

Free offer: Baby's Book

see plate 171

1952

This picture was produced on a solid pewter pendant for National Baby Week in 1979.

See plate 66, page 136

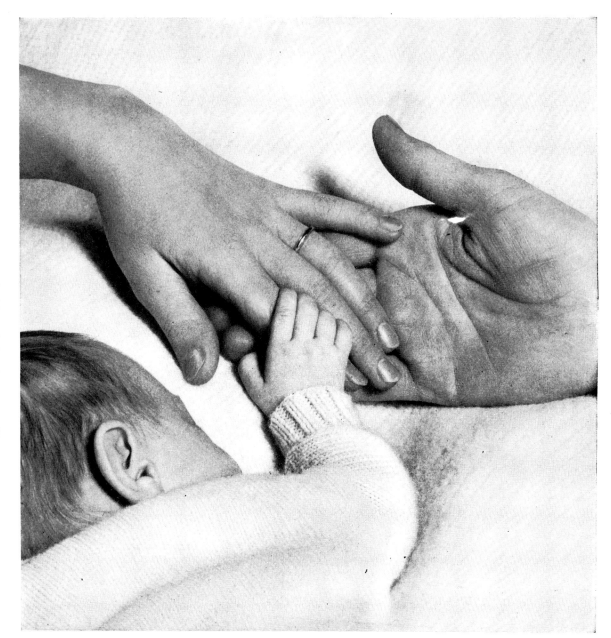

the Future
in your hands

Instinctively, the tiny fingers grasp yours. The gesture shows your baby's complete confidence in you. He trusts you to give him the tenderness that makes a happy heart . . . the encouragement that makes a lively mind . . . the care that makes a sturdy body.

Babies are our business... our only business!

Gerber's BABY FOODS

4 CEREALS • 40 STRAINED AND JUNIOR FOODS • 10 MEATS

Bringing Up Baby

HINTS COLLECTED BY

Mrs. Dan Gerber

(MOTHER OF 5)

Mrs. Gerber

Menu Suggestions. Little ones like varied meals, too. So Gerber's try to make it pleasant for them and easy for Mommy. Tiniest ones might have rice cereal and applesauce. Babies who've reached the meat-potato-vegetable stage also find Gerber's can fill the bill o' fare! Say, strained beef, sweet potatoes, beets—topped off with pears and pineapple (and milk or formula, of course). Or strained lamb, squash, green beans, and custard pudding. If you look at the attractive true color of all of them, you just know they're bound to have true flavor, too.

* * *

Lukewarm — that's the right temperature for baby's drinking water. Be very careful with it: Boil it, always—and use only sterilized bottles.

* * *

Accepted—by the Council on Foods and Nutrition of the American Medical Association—*all* of Gerber's Baby Foods. That includes such Gerber favorites as sweet potatoes, beef heart, orange pudding. A gratifying note for young mothers.

* * *

Bread-and-Butter Note. Ever make sandwiches for between-meal snacks? Mothers who try to keep sweets from overcrowding the menu often use strained peaches or apricot-applesauce in place of jam or jelly.

FREE! "Foods for Baby and Mealtime Psychology"—a 32-page booklet overflowing with expert advice compiled for you by Gerber's baby foods specialists. Just write to me, Mrs. Dan Gerber, Dept. 14-2, Fremont, Mich. In Canada, Gerber-Ogilvie Baby Foods Ltd., Niagara Falls, Canada.

Women's Day 1952

An updated picture of Mrs. Gerber accompanies her column.

Free book offer: <u>Foods for Baby Mealtime Psychology</u>

See plate 181, page 163

Plum good eating!

Picture the finest of rosy-purple, juicy-sweet plums . . . picked at tree-ripened perfection . . . blended into a delicious fruit-dessert, especially textured for your baby! That's Gerber's Plums with Tapioca! Such good eating that Gerber's make both strained and junior versions for babies of all ages to enjoy.

Plums with tapioca give only a sampling of Gerber's whole delicious variety of baby foods. For Gerber's have created a really *complete* range for your baby—cereals, fruits, vegetables, soups, desserts . . . even meats.

Every single one is made from expertly selected ingredients, skillfully processed to conserve nutrients to the fullest extent possible by modern methods. And every single one of Gerber's more than 50 varieties has the superb quality you'd expect from people who make baby foods and nothing else.

Babies are our business . . . our only business!

Gerber's
BABY FOODS

CEREALS • STRAINED AND JUNIOR FOODS • MEATS

Bringing Up Baby

HINTS COLLECTED BY

Mrs Dan Gerber

(MOTHER OF 5)

Mrs. Gerber

Am I Real? Week after week, mail comes in to ask if I'm a "made up" person or if I actually exist. If you could see our house at times when our two married children come a-visiting with their babies, and our three younger children come in from school with some of their friends—well, I don't think there'd be much doubt as to how real this whole lively family is! (There are also two very real, lively dogs and two very real, lively cats on the premises.)

*　　*　　*

NATIONAL BABY WEEK
APRIL 26 – MAY 3

This is a good time to double-check your grocer's shelves. You may be surprised to realize exactly how many things he has to help you with baby's needs. All those delicious Gerber's Baby Foods, for instance—from starting cereals through a wonderful variety of strained and junior foods.

You might double-check your own shelves to make sure you've the wide choice that makes eating interesting and fun for your little one. Another good thing to check: first-aid supplies for small accidents. And then how about intangibles – such as making sure *both* you and Daddy have plenty of time to encourage that extraclose, friendly relationship so important to baby.

*　　*　　*

Good Start — Free! Samples of Gerber's Rice Cereal, Barley Cereal, Oatmeal, and Cereal Food (wheat). Just write me, Mrs. Dan Gerber, Dept. 15-2, Fremont, Michigan. In Canada, Gerber-Ogilvie Baby Foods Ltd., Niagara Falls, Canada.

Off to a Good Start!

When the time comes for baby's first spoon-fed food, you naturally want to make it a happy occasion for both of you. That's why Gerber's make a special effort to offer you starting foods with texture that appeals to baby, and flavor that helps develop his sense of taste. Then he's off to a good start in eating habits!

For example, there are four starting cereals: Gerber's Rice Cereal—the *original* ready-to-serve rice cereal for babies—plus Gerber's Barley Cereal, Oatmeal, and Cereal Food (wheat). All are enriched with B-vitamins and minerals . . . all are pre-cooked.

Among the thirty strained foods are such "early" favorites as Gerber's Pears, Peas, Beef . . . all processed for high retention of nutritive values. And all with the true color and true flavor that babies prefer.

Whatever varieties your doctor recommends, you can turn to Gerber's with confidence—knowing that Gerber's make baby foods and nothing else!

Babies are our business...
our only business!

Gerber's BABY FOODS

CEREALS • STRAINED AND JUNIOR FOODS • MEATS

3

180

a Good Beginning is _so_ Important!

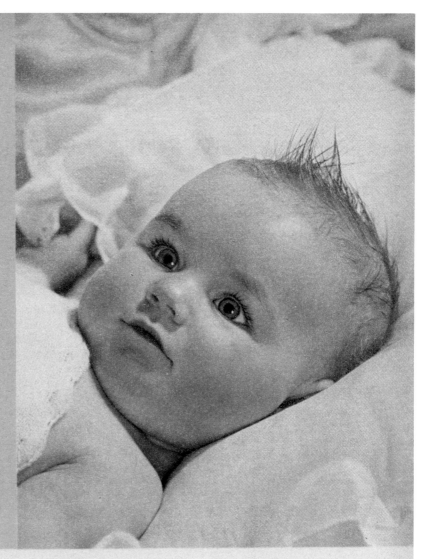

HOME from the hospital . . . and suddenly you know baby is _really_ yours. From here on, you hold the key to his future well-being. Now your heart will speak for you—in the special language that only a baby understands. Now your hands will work with a new devotion—the kind that makes a baby blossom.

EARLY devotion to baby's physical needs is important, too! That's why Gerber's make every effort to provide starting foods which are particularly pleasing to delicate palates, yet offer the nourishing qualities growing bodies need.

As your baby progresses to something more than an all-liquid diet, a variety of well-balanced meals becomes important in helping baby build future good-eating habits. Gerber's _complete_ selection of strained foods makes it ever so easy to keep appetite interest alive.

FIRST-OFF, there are Gerber's "Starters"— 4 Cereals, Orange Juice, Egg Yolks and Meats—foods usually suggested by doctors for little beginners.

The pre-cooked Baby Cereals have the bland, but distinctive, flavors babies prefer—are smooth-textured—vitamin- and mineral-enriched. (Now in the new "Quad" package—small-size boxes of Rice, Barley, Oatmeal and Cereal Food—all wrapped together for easy use.)

Gerber's Strained Orange Juice has a mild, natural flavor and high vitamin-C content. Then come the custard-smooth Strained Egg Yolks, extra-rich in vitamin-A and iron.

For the complete body-building proteins your growing baby needs, Gerber's offer 7 savory, Strained Meats. Made of selected Armour Cuts, they're all meat, with just enough broth added to give a pleasant, easy-to-swallow texture.

TO FURTHER THE CAUSE of a well-balanced diet: Gerber's Strained Fruits, Vegetables and Soups—famous for their tempting true flavors, appealing natural colors and nice-on-the-tongue texture. To round out the appetizing picture: Gerber's delicious, nutritious Desserts.

4 CEREALS • 60 STRAINED & JUNIOR FOODS, INCLUDING MEATS

Babies are our business... our only business!

Gerber's
BABY FOODS

ARMOUR

Gerber's Baby Foods, Fremont, Mich., Oakland, Cal., Rochester, N. Y., Niagara Falls, Canada

Family Circle 1954- Note the picture of the Gerber Quads- the free samples given for writing into the company.

BRINGING UP BABY®

Hints collected by Mrs. Dan Gerber *mother of five...*

Sure a baby means hard work! But don't forget that a baby is fun and thrives on fun. So *make* time to play with your pride 'n joy. *Take* time to chat, cuddle, croon, clap hands or whatever. And try these commonsensible hints on for size.

Do shrug off those drudge tasks once in awhile to romp with baby for the sheer joy of it. Dusting can wait. A little heart that wants to dance often can't.

Do make a point of smiling often. Be surprised how often you get smiled back at . . . what a morale-booster it is for both baby and you.

Accepted with pleasure. There are usually coos of approval on the part of wee ones when you serve Gerber Strained Foods. For these good-tasting fruits, vegetables, soups, meats and desserts are carefully cooked, mildly seasoned and smoothly pureed to  please delicate taste buds and tummies. More than that, they're specially prepared to preserve naturally good flavors, appetizing colors and a high degree of wholesome food values. 38 varieties for imaginative mealtime planning.

More dietary data. Important trio for a small-fry diet: delicate Gerber Strained Orange Juice, for consistently high vitamin C — Strained Egg Yolks for iron and vitamin A — Strained Bananas for energy-giving calories.

Spotless tactic. Sheet plastic, thumb-tacked to the top of baby's dresser, spares the wood from stains. Add a bright ribbon edging for a festive touch. Important: tacks should be placed *under* edge of top.

Straight story with an old wrinkle. Raveled yarn can be easily straightened for re-use if you wind it around a slab of sturdy cardboard and give it a quick dunk in lukewarm water. When dry, the wool will be straight as a die and ready for new knitting.

Most little ones take to the taste of meat right from the start. Gerber Strained Meats are famous for savory true-meat  flavors. Made from selected Armour cuts, they're processed to remove most of the fat and fiber. That's why even tiny babies can digest them easily. Nutritionally speaking, they're rich in the complete proteins so necessary for growth, strength and the development of all body structures. Your choice of 8 varieties — all 100% meat with just enough broth to give a pleasant-feeling texture.

ARMOUR

Set for the sandman, honey?
With your GERBER BABY DOLL
a-cuddle? Sleep sweetly!

Get this charming replica of the famous Gerber Baby for your darling. A $3.75 value for only $2.00 and 6 Gerber Baby Food labels or cereal box tops. 12 in. high, it drinks, wets, cries, sits up — has movable arms and legs. Complete with play accessories. Mail money and labels to Gerber Baby Foods, Dept. 110-5, Fremont, Mich. In Canada: Box 68, Toronto 18. Good only in U. S. A., its possessions and Canada. Expires Dec. 31, 1955.

Babies are our business... our only business!  **Gerber**® BABY FOODS

4 CEREALS • OVER 65 STRAINED AND JUNIOR FOODS, INCLUDING MEATS

1955 ad for first Gerber Baby doll Premium offer. See plate 5, page 21

bringing up baby

Hints collected by Mrs. Dan Gerber, mother of five...

Mrs. Dan Gerber

Half the fun of making New Year's resolutions is breaking them, they say. But no one will deny that these self-promises (lived up to or not) are good for the soul. However, they're more apt to be kept if you don't aim for the impossible. How about trying on these suggestions for size?

I shall try to remember that:

My baby has rights — and that loving away lonesomeness is more important than rearranging the kitchen cupboard.

My husband has rights — and deserves a full share of attention too! (And I'll not neglect those little primp-ups that make him proud of me.)

I have rights — and will make the budget stretch to include a baby sitter periodically.

Inside story. Do hoard gay gift-wrappings. They make such cheerful, colorful drawer liners for baby's wardrobe chest.

Undercover story. A sprinkling of baby's powder under those drawer-liners will lend a pleasant fragrance to baby's togs.

No matter what the season, your baby can always enjoy good-tasting, fresh-flavored fruits and vegetables. Gerber Strained Peaches or Apricots, say. Succulent Strained Squash or Creamed Spinach, for instance. Because Gerber Strained Fruits and Vegetables are picked and packed at the peak of their growing seasons. Naturally they're carefully cleaned and specially cooked to preserve true-to-nature flavors and eye-appealing colors — as well as wholesome food values. Your choice of 9 luscious fruits — 9 tasty vegetables.

Have you tried a spoonful of Gerber Strained Egg Yolks as a sunny, creamy topping for one of baby's green vegetables? Delicious!

Timely comment. These wintry days, the best time to air your little heir (or heiress) is between 10 A.M. and 2 P.M. Daily ex-

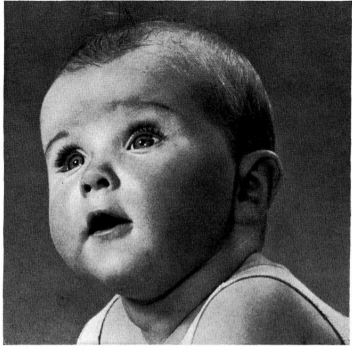

Better Living- 1956

Ad for free picture of the Gerber Baby.

cursions should not be skipped except in unusually bad weather.

Basic idea. All through the early years, cereals are basic in the infant menu. Gerber Cereals are specially prepared to suit the likes and needs of little ones. Rice, Barley, Oatmeal and Cereal Food (a mixed cereal) provide bland but distinctive flavors that appeal to young taste buds. All four have the creamy texture that feels especially pleasant. You simply add milk, formula or other liquids — stir to smoothness and serve. From a nutritional standpoint — each one is fortified with blood-building iron, bone-building calcium and important B-vitamins to more than whole grain value. Gerber Cereals come in large-size packages with handy, spill-proof pouring spout. Or in the small-size, 4 in 1 "Quad" package, so baby can enjoy variety.

Can't you picture it! If you would like a print of the endearing Gerber Baby, suitable for framing, just send 10¢ (to cover cost of handling) to Mrs. Dan Gerber, Dept. 671-6, Fremont, Mich.

4 cereals—over 65 strained and junior foods including meats

Babies are our business... our only business!

Gerber
BABY FOODS

bringing up baby.

Hints collected by Mrs. Dan Gerber mother of five...

1956

Free book offer – "Recipes for Toddlers"

First available in 1952

See plate 28, page 126

Although most toddlers dearly love to eat, some of them do get choosey from time to time. If your child is going through a pick 'n choose period, try not to fuss, but do vary menus more. Substitute foods he (or she) likes for those he doesn't. After a bit try re-introducing the rejected items: Chances are Junior will have forgotten those self-styled prejudices and lick the platter clean.

Profitable sharing plan. Eating alone isn't much fun. Toddlers are sociable beings, and often eat better when mother shares the same bill of fare. So why not try a mother-toddler luncheon? Fun for both baby and you — cuts down food preparation too.

Meat Pie*
Gerber Junior
Creamed Spinach
Gerber
Junior Applesauce
Graham Crackers
Milk—Coffee or Tea
for you

*MEAT PIE

| 1 container Gerber Junior Beef, Veal or Pork | ¾ cup mashed potato |

Butter small casserole. Place half the mashed potato in bottom. Top with meat. Spoon remainder of potato in mounds around edge of casserole, leaving a bit of meat showing in center. Bake at (375°F) until lightly browned.
Season to individual taste.

More menu ideas for one or two. Gerber's "Recipes for Toddlers" is yours for the asking. Write me, Dept. 192-6, Fremont, Mich.

Short cut to longer life for little girls' dresses. Snip off part of the skirts — hem tops and use them for blouses under little jumpers. They're charming.

Brush-up lesson. Corduroy overalls look better, last longer when you don't iron them. While overalls are still damp, brush the pile in one direction to keep the corduroy fluffy and new looking.

Meat-y facts. Active toddlers not only get a good satisfied feeling from meat, but this important food provides the complete proteins vital to growth, strength and muscle development. Gerber Junior Meats are made from selected Armour cuts — carefully prepared to remove almost all the fat and fiber and preserve Armour true-meat goodness. All five are 100% meat, chopped into tender, evenly-minced bits that tots with a few teeth **ARMOUR** can manage easily.

Match trick. More than one little tot in the house? Try initialing little socks on the bottom with indelible ink. Makes it easier to match and mate socks when sorting clean laundry.

Simply delicious. That's the way to describe the new Gerber Junior Chicken Noodle Dinner. Delicate chicken, fluffy egg noodles and bright carrot bits are all happily combined with savory chicken broth. Truly a flavorful dish for your darling.

Toothsome idea that's wholesome too! Gerber Teething Biscuits are made of enriched cereal — baked extra hard to provide biting exercise and soothing relief for tender gums.

Babies are our business... our only business!

Gerber ®BABY FOODS

4 CEREALS • OVER 65 STRAINED AND JUNIOR FOODS, INCLUDING MEATS

bringing up baby.

Hints Collected
by Mrs. Dan Gerber,
Mother of five

Wise observation from a proud new grandmother: "Times certainly have changed where baby feeding is concerned. These days we know so much more about the need for vitamins, minerals, proteins and the like, it's small wonder our modern babies blossom as they do. But one thing hasn't changed a whit. A baby's need for love. Just as important as nourishing food is plain old-fashioned mother love. May not show up in inches and ounces, but it sure makes a baby grow and glow inside."

Nutrition notation. Speaking of vitamins and minerals, did you know that Gerber Strained Foods are specially pressure-processed to preserve vital food values and the *naturally* good true flavors so often lost in home cooking? (Cooking in the absence of air does it.) And Gerber offers you a far wider variety than you could prepare economically at home. Over 35 Strained Fruits, Vegetables, Soups, Meats and Desserts—more ways to satisfy little appetites than you can shake a spoon at. All pureed to a good-feeling smoothness, and mildly seasoned to suit unsophisticated taste buds.

2 fruit-ful ideas for you. Borrow some of baby's strained peaches, plums or pears:

1. **For breakfast** — spoon generously on waffles, pancakes or hot cereal.

2. **For lunch** —blend 2 tablespoons of any Gerber Strained Fruit with peanut butter or cream cheese. Tempting on whole-wheat bread or toast.

Lotion notion. A column-reading mother writes: "I toss baby's plastic lotion bottle right into the bath with her. Warms the lotion just enough to make it feel extra-pleasant."

Variety makes for a happy taste of affairs where small fry are concerned. Gerber Cereal Quads provide four good-tasting ways to stimulate mealtime zeal. Handy 4-in-1 package contains small boxes of enriched Rice, Barley, Oatmeal and Cereal Food (a mixed cereal) for easy rotation of cereal variety.

P. S. Save the bright-colored Quad boxes and string 'em between the bars of baby's play pen. Fun to push and pull—fun to smile back at the friendly Gerber Baby.

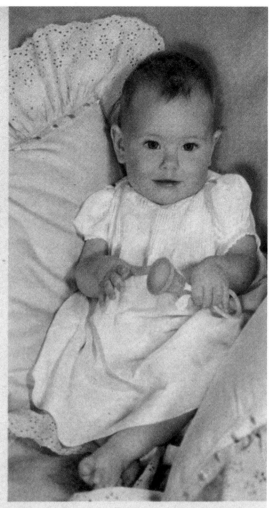

Family Circle - 1956

Repeat of 1955 premium offer for Sun Rubber Gerber Baby Doll

FEATURE OF THE MONTH

A CUE FOR CHRISTMAS—Get your angel a GERBER BABY DOLL. It's a $3.75 VALUE for only $2.25 and 6 Gerber labels or cereal box tops. This charming 12 in. replica of the Gerber Baby drinks, wets, cries, sits up — has movable arms and legs. Soft vinyl head and rubber body make it completely safe. Comes with diaper, bib, bottle and oatmeal playbox.

Mail money and labels to Gerber Baby Foods, Dept. 1910-6, Fremont, Mich. In Canada: Box 4027, Terminal A, Toronto, Ont. Offer good only in U.S.A. and Canada. Expires June 30, 1957.

Babies are our business . . . our *only* business!

BABY FOODS
FREMONT, MICHIGAN

4 CEREALS • OVER 70 STRAINED AND
JUNIOR FOODS, INCLUDING MEATS

bringing up baby.

HINTS COLLECTED BY MRS. DAN GERBER, MOTHER OF 5

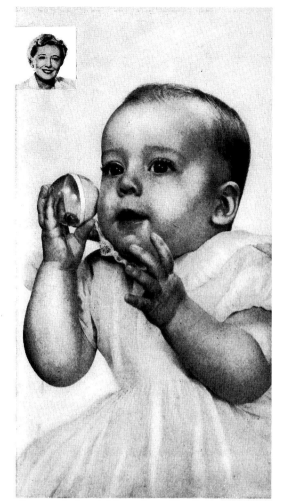

A FATHER SPEAKS UP. From time to time I like to get a father's slant on baby care. Recently I talked to the father of two happy, well-adjusted children, and I asked him what he thought were the best guides to good parenthood. Without a moment's hesitation he said: "Patience, perception and playfulness." Can't think of a more intelligent point of view, can you?

FEATURE OF THE MONTH *(Santa Claus Suggestion)*.
The perfect Christmas gift for toddlers: the exclusive Gerber Baby Doll. It's a $3.75 value for only $2.00 and 6 Gerber Baby Food labels or Cereal boxtops. This charming replica of the famous Gerber Baby is 12″ high and as versatile as tykes like a baby doll to be. It cries, drinks, wets, sits up — has movable arms and legs. Soft vinyl head and rubber body makes it completely safe and washable. Comes complete with play accessories for added fun.

For your Gerber Baby Doll, just mail $2.00 and labels to Gerber Baby Foods, Dept. 410-8, Fremont, Mich. (In Canada: Gerber Baby Foods, Box 4027, Terminal "A", Toronto.) Offer expires June 30, 1959.

DO-IT-YOURSELF HAPPINESS. An older baby will often be more content in his playpen if you give him a few toys that make him do something with his hands.

• Slip a bright, small toy in a plastic bag. Baby will be able to see that something's inside . . . have a lot of fun trying to get it out.

• A gaily-colored scarf, tied loosely to one of the pen bars is fun to look at . . . fun to try to untie.

• Empty, small-size cereal boxes, strung between the bars, are swell for punching and pulling.

YOU CAN BE "CHOOSE-Y." No one food is worth making a "scene" over when you have so many Gerber Strained Foods in every category to choose from. Gerber offers over 45 fruits, vegetables, meats, soups, meat dinners and desserts. All are specially processed to preserve tempting colors, natural flavors and the utmost in nutritive values. All are quality tested in 28 ways — for when it comes to babies . . . mothers and Gerber agree, it's quality first. P.S. Has baby tried the newest Gerber goody: Turkey with Vegetables?

Meet my darling, bright-eyed granddaughter — Gay McClintock Phinny, youngest of my daughter Sally's four children. Sally was the original Gerber Baby — and Gay follows happily in her mother's footsteps.

Gerber ®

BABY FOODS
FREMONT, MICHIGAN

BABIES ARE OUR BUSINESS . . . OUR ONLY BUSINESS!

5 CEREALS · OVER 85 STRAINED & JUNIOR FOODS, INCLUDING MEATS

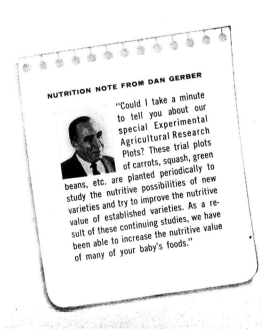

NUTRITION NOTE FROM DAN GERBER
"Could I take a minute to tell you about our special Experimental Agricultural Research Plots? These trial plots of carrots, squash, green beans, etc. are planted periodically to study the nutritive possibilities of new varieties and try to improve the nutritive value of established varieties. As a result of these continuing studies, we have been able to increase the nutritive value of many of your baby's foods."

Good Housekeeping 1958- This ad has three members of the Gerber family, Mr. & Mrs. Dan Gerber and grandaughter, Gay. Also, an ad extending the offer for the premium Sun Rubber Doll to 6-30-59.

bringing up baby®
*Hints collected by Mrs. Dan Gerber,
Mother of 5*

How to find out what fingers are for

Busy fingers begin to become aware of their usefulness at about the age of 3 or 4 months. Wonderful how baby discovers that fingers are fine for getting the feel of everything from ears to toes . . . toys to clothes. At 6 or 7 months he uses them to grasp and hold his bottle. 8 or 9 months find those fingers transferring toys from one hand to another . . . and oh, magic moment, at 1 year he can usually pick up small objects with thumb and forefinger.

If baby scoops up his food
with his fingers, what matter if it's a bit messy? Rejoice in the fact that he's learning hand control and soon will be able to make a spoon behave. Babies delight in Gerber Junior Foods because they have a flair for flavor. Mothers delight in them because they're so nourishing. Over 40 varieties, specially prepared to preserve the utmost in precious food values. Why not stimulate mealtime interest by rotating colors and kinds of foods?

Have you treated baby
to Gerber Junior Pears and Pineapple, Ham with Vegetables or Creamed Cottage Cheese with Pineapple?

New! Educational, too!
Finger feeders can practice hand-to-mouth coordination with Gerber Cookies with added protein . . . now in adorable animal shapes. Nutritionally speaking, they have twice as much protein as most other cookies, plus B-vitamins in the icing. Fun to eat, fun way to teach baby animal names. Serve with any Gerber Fruit or Gerber Juice.

Tiny hands learn from take-apart and put-together playthings such as nesting toys, educational fit-together toys, building blocks . . . all designed to teach coordination and control.

FOR FREE, COLORFUL REPRINT OF THIS CHARMING LITTLE LASS, WRITE TO GERBER BABY FOODS, DEPT. 1910-1, FREMONT, MICHIGAN

Important: Gerber prepares over 100 baby foods: cereals, strained and junior, to meet your baby's nutritional needs. We're proud to say:

"Babies are our business...our only business!"®

1961- Offer for free print of this charming little girl plate 102, page 144. Lithographed Juice can Plate 25, page 126.

187

How nice! It's Baby Week

For colorful reprint of this little charmer, write to: Gerber Baby Foods, Dept. 73-BW, Fremont, Michigan.

HAROLD HALMA

And how nice it is to belong to a baby! A baby can bestir you to smile when you don't think you can. Send your heart a-soaring when it's in a slump. Call back your dreams. Sweeten your sense of humor.

Yes, a baby brightens our days in so many ways the rewards cannot be measured. Cause enough for dedicating a week to babies.

Baby Week bulletin

How nice, too, that there are so many fine products designed for your baby's comfort, pleasure and nutritional well-being.

During Baby Week (April 30-May 7) the beguiling "Little Girl Blue" in the picture will be greeting you in supermarkets everywhere…guiding you to the many wonderful values your grocer will be featuring. Look for her. She'll be waiting for you.

Good news for your baby

Now, in addition to all the good-tasting foods for babies from the infant age to the toddler stage, Gerber brings you durable and oh-so-comfortable babywear.

There are cotton shirts, socks, training pants, crib sheets and nylon stretch socks. All dazzle-white, downy soft, machine washable and driable. And, the new Gerber Babywear is quality-controlled according to the strict standards that have made Gerber so famous.

For your convenience, you'll be happy to know these new Gerber products are sold in supermarkets. [P.S.] You'll also find sturdy, waterproof, plastic Gerber Baby Pants and Bibs there too.

Mealtime success story

Service with a smile puts delight in every bite. If you let baby eat instead of urging him to eat, enjoyment of food will come naturally.

New ways to sweeten eatin' time

Top off baby's meal with one of the new Gerber Desserts…Dutch Apple Dessert or Cherry-Vanilla Pudding…both great. Dutch Apple is a delicious, applesaucy dessert, made extra-delectable with butter and a bright, light touch of cinnamon. Nutritionally, it's enriched with Vitamin C.

Cherry-Vanilla is a pleasant-tasting pudding made with egg yolks and other wholesome ingredients.

Nutrition note: Gerber prepares over 100 baby foods—infant formulas, cereals, strained and junior foods—to meet your baby's nutritional needs. We're proud to say:

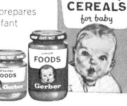

"Babies are our business… our only business!"®

GERBER® PRODUCTS COMPANY, BOX 72, FREMONT, MICHIGAN

Family Circle 1963- The most popular ad ever printed offered a free picture of this little girl in blue.
The offer was good through 1966. Plate 103, page 145

2-way stretch, 3-ply thread, multiple stitching...the important "extras" in Gerber De Luxe Training Pants

To fit snugly without binding, your baby's training pants must have some "give." Gerber De Luxe Training Pants have permanent give, with 2-way stretch. When your baby bends, stoops, squats, runs, plays—they bend as he does, and fit perfectly.

They're soft and fine to the touch. 100% combed cotton is closely knit. You may be sure they won't sag or shrink out of fit—no matter how often they're washed and dried.

Important features: Triple fabric crotch, double-thick front and back panels assure greater absorbency and extra wear. 4 needles join the panels with 3-ply thread. 3 needles attach the waist. 9 threads are used at "strain" points to give the pants longer life.

Heat-resistant elastic at both legs and waist is not affected by the heat of the dryer. So until baby outgrows them, his Gerber De Luxe Training Pants will give superb fit, from waist to legs and all around, however active he is.

Gerber De Luxe
Training Pants
—1 to 3 years.

Gerber Baby Shirts.
Pull-ons–6 mos.
to 3 yrs. Snap-ons–
3 mos. to 1½ yrs.
(Diaper Tapes on all
shirts to 1½ yrs.)

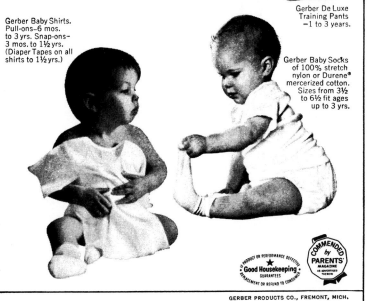

Gerber Baby Socks
of 100% stretch
nylon or Durene®
mercerized cotton.
Sizes from 3½
to 6½ fit ages
up to 3 yrs.

Good Housekeeping GUARANTEES

COMMENDED by PARENTS' MAGAZINE

GERBER PRODUCTS CO., FREMONT, MICH.

1965

An ad for Gerber Baby Wear

See Plate 7, page 120

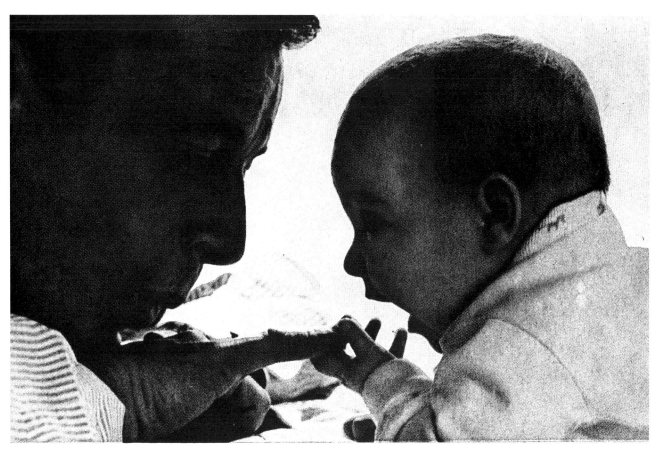

Pat-a-cake, pat-a-cake, baker's man...The games Daddy plays with Baby are an important part of Baby's well-being.

Mrs. Dan Gerber
Mother of Five

Long before baby can pat-a-cake or peek-a-boo he or she can bounce on Daddy's knee. And enjoy such simple "games" as playing with Daddy's hand — or his necktie.

The closer Daddy and baby are, the happier is baby. And Daddy!

When Daddy feeds baby

That, too, brings Daddy and baby closer together. For a weekend cereal feeding, Daddy-style, how about Gerber® Cereals with Fruit, in the jar? Ready to serve.

Rice Cereal, Oatmeal or Mixed Cereal, with applesauce and bananas for delicate flavor. Important B-vitamins in each.

Suited to a baby's taste

Are your taste and baby's the same? Most physicians and child psychologists think not. That's the reason for the extensive Gerber program of product testing by babies in the babies' own homes.

We process vegetables and fruits at the peak of *natural* flavor. Gerber Sweet Potatoes, for instance, are given a *slow-cook* to develop their natural sweetness to suit *baby's* taste.

Baby's best friend

If you're in doubt about when to start baby on a new food, your baby's doctor is the one to ask.

As the baby specialists, we too rely regularly on the guidance of the medical profession. As a matter of fact, among numerous professional consultants, we have a pediatrician on our Board of Directors. That's the extra assurance you get when you buy Gerber foods for your baby.

Sweet Potato Custard

(A toddler treat Dad might like, too!)

1 jar Gerber Strained Sweet Potatoes
1 egg, *slightly beaten* • ½ tsp. sugar
½ tsp. butter or margarine, melted
Salt, to taste • Bits of crisp bacon

Combine all ingredients except bacon. Pour into 2 greased custard cups and place in gently boiling water. Cover and cook 20 minutes. Sprinkle bacon over and serve. Gerber Sweet Potatoes, like Gerber Carrots, are high in vitamin-A value.

Important: Gerber has 127 nourishing foods, created *especially* for baby.

Babywear, too. Durable, dependable... yet comfy and soft.

Babies are our business... our only business!®

Gerber Baby Products, Box 33, Fremont, Michigan 49412

1968- Good Housekeeping. An updated picture of Mrs. Dan Gerber. This ad shows the father playing an important role in baby's care. Also, note the products carry the Good Housekeeping Seal of Approval.

**Gerber® prepares Toddler Meals
for the most important person
in the world...your baby.**

WE PREPARE Toddler Meals for babies who aren't quite babies any more. Youngsters who are starting to outgrow baby food, but can't always eat what you do. A convenient Toddler Meal, served with milk and fruit or dessert, offers your baby a complete nutritious meal – while he learns to feed himself.

Gerber Beef Stew combines bite-size pieces of lean beef and bright vegetables to give your toddler nourishment and enjoyment. It provides important protein and gives you a wonderful value in nutrition and convenience.

Gerber Lasagna is a tasty blend of meat, cheese and pasta in a special sauce. It's lightly seasoned for toddlers and cut up into bite-size pieces. A great way to introduce your youngster to new kinds of foods.

Babies are our business...
Gerber Products Co., Fremont, Mich. 49412

FAMILY FOOD IDEAS

1971- Note slogan change It has been shortened to Babies are Our Business... as food products were produced for toddlers.

Gerber®: more kinds of cereals for more kinds of nourishment.

Gerber Rice Cereal with Strawberries is a brand new flavor. It has the iron and vitamin enrichment of regular Rice Cereal...plus the summer-sweet taste of real strawberries.

New Gerber Rice Cereal with Strawberries is just one of nine different cereals we prepare, to give you more ways to give your baby the nourishment he needs. From the five regular pre-cooked cereals...to three cereal-fruit combinations...to cereals with applesauce and bananas in jars. Many in a variety of sizes too, from one-ounce boxes (in Cereal "Sixes") to 16-oz. packages. Small wonder more mothers look to Gerber cereals for the kind of nourishment—and variety—their babies need.

Special Baby Week Offer: Each set (four colorful plastic cereal bowls and four cups) only 50¢ with one boxtop from any Gerber Cereal with Fruit.

Send order to:

Bowl & Cup Offer
P.O. Box 800, Fremont, Michigan 49412

Please send me _____ breakfast sets. For each set ordered, I enclose 50¢ and one boxtop from any Gerber Cereal with Fruit.

Name _____ (Please print) _____

Address _____

City _____

State _____ Zip _____

Babies are our business...
Please allow 4 weeks for delivery. Offer good in U.S.A., except where restricted or prohibited by law. Offer expires Sept. 30, 1971.

39

1971- Premium offer for tumbler and bowl set. See, Plate 16, page 123.

your baby with love.

Nursing him...
Nursing your baby is like sharing love. And Gerber gives you more time to enjoy it. Our new nurser bags have tabs that make each bag easy to open and provide a nice snug fit. And the tapered shape of the bag fits all popular nursers. No adapter necessary. The bags even have ounce markings printed right on them so you can see how much formula baby has taken.

Feeding him...
Gerber has been helping to feed babies since you were a baby. Today Gerber offers over 150 different foods—cereals, juices, strained and junior foods, and toddler meals. All prepared with one thought in mind: to help provide your baby with proper nourishment for a healthier future.

Clothing him...
You'll find little "extras" in babywear that carries the Gerber name. Like bind-free seamless underarms in our cotton shirts. And nylon finished edges on our vinyl pants. Our stretch socks really stretch. Your baby may outgrow Gerber babywear, but chances are he'll never outwear it.

And Babygro® by Gerber sleepwear is flame retardant. You'll find it in leading department stores and infant specialty shops.

Soothing him...
Gerber also takes special care of baby in the nursery, with vaporizer-humidifiers that provide comfort whenever it's needed. A vaporizer-humidifier not only helps relieve colds' discomforts, it also adds moisture to dry indoor air. Hankscraft makes a full line of compact models... with safety features that will be comforting to you, too.

Protecting him...
Gerber Life, a separate subsidiary of Gerber Products Company, offers low-cost insurance protection to young, growing families. And at the time when they need it the most but can afford it the least. Many different plans to choose from—protecting one member of your family or all of them. At rates that are budget priced.

Now, more than ever, Gerber helps surround your baby with love.

Gerber

Gerber Products Company, Fremont, Michigan 49412

Is your baby really ready for table food?

The "right time" for table food depends on your baby's individual needs, and, of course, your doctor's recommendation. But even then, there will be meals you prepare for the rest of the family that may not be right for your baby. They're possibly too spicy. Or not nutritious enough. Or the texture isn't quite right.

For these times, there's still a place for Gerber in your baby's menu.

The bridge to table food.
Gerber junior foods are specially prepared for this important stage in your baby's development. They not only provide more "grown-up" flavors and textures, but also assure you of serving your baby foods that are safe, pure and wholesome.

Gerber offers a wide variety of foods for the junior-sized appetite — fruits, meats, dinners and vegetables (many of your baby's favorite Gerber strained foods are also available in junior texture). And, of course, Gerber iron-enriched cereals, to help protect against iron deficiency all through the first and even second year.

Eat the basic 4 foods every day.

Gerber vegetable-and-meat combinations are economical sources of meat protein. And Gerber High Meat Dinners, with 30% or more meat, by weight, will provide your baby with nearly one-third of the recommended daily allowance for protein.

The toddler age.
Even when your baby has started on table foods, you'll find occasions for serving Gerber Toddler Meals. A convenient Toddler Meal, ideal for ages 1 to 4, served with milk and fruit, is a complete, nutritious lunch or supper.

Our pull-on shirts won't shrink out of fit, no matter how often you wash them.
Gerber knit shirts are made to take the tugs and twists that go with an active baby's life. Made of 100% combed cotton, they're specially treated to minimize shrinkage, through countless trips through washer and dryer. Gerber stretch nylon socks, too, have long-lasting shape, and stretch to fit wiggling toes.

Babies are our business...

Gerber

Gerber Products Company, Fremont, Mich. 49412

1975- Note the ads for baby wear and junior foods.

Gerber helps surround

1975- Two page ad featuring the extended line of Gerber Products.

A mother's confidence is earned with Quality and Concern.

A mother's confidence is not given freely and that's as it should be. At Gerber, we continue to earn this trust by adding quality and concern to every product we make. We've been doing it for fifty years.

Gerber baby foods contain only wholesome ingredients. Selected and prepared under Gerber's high standards. And that's just the beginning.

Gerber pioneered the reduction of sugar and in 1977 stopped adding salt to baby foods.

Sugar is an important source of energy for your baby. And in most cases, the natural sugars found in many foods are sufficient to meet your baby's needs. That's why Gerber adds sugar (in carefully controlled amounts) to only those few foods that require additional sweetening, like tart fruits and desserts. We started this program to minimize the use of added sugar in 1972, becoming the first baby company to do so.

In 1977, all baby food companies, including Gerber, stopped adding salt to baby

foods. We did this because the pediatric experts are unable to specify the ideal salt intake and some parents expressed a desire for baby foods without added salt. Some of our "no salt added" products are on your grocer's shelf now and the others will be there soon.

Our label tells the whole story.

The Gerber label is made very clear, on purpose. We are proud of what goes into every jar and we

This product contributes essential nutrients.
It was prepared without added:
Salt • Sugar • Preservatives
Artificial Flavors or Colors
MSG or other flavor enhancers

want you to know what goes into your baby. As a matter of fact, there are only two ingredients we don't mention on our labels. They are the *Quality* and *Concern* we have added to our products for the last 50 years.

STRAINED BABY FOODS
NO SALT ADDED
Gerber

Gerber
Fifty Years of Caring
Gerber Products Company, Fremont, MI 49412

1978- In honor of the 50th Anniversary Year the slogan reads "Gerber- Fifty Years of Caring".

How can I supplement my baby's diet without interfering with breast feeding?

Breast-fed babies are very fortunate. They receive a sound nutritional start, and the special closeness of breast feeding is a wonderful foundation for a secure and loving relationship.

It's no wonder that many breast-feeding mothers are reluctant to introduce bottle fed formula when the time comes to supplement breast milk. When bottle feedings fulfill baby's need to suckle, breast milk stimulation diminishes, and the nursing experience may be foreshortened.

By spoon feeding Gerber Baby Foods, you can add needed nutrients to your baby's diet and begin an important developmental step with no interference to suckling. Spoon feeding provides baby with new tastes and textures, new stimulation, and a new opportunity to socialize that does not hamper or replace nursing.

The addition of wholesome Gerber foods can help meet your baby's growing nutrient needs while you continue to nurse.

STRAINED CARROTS

Gerber

NET WT. 4 1/2 OZ. (128 GMS)

®Gerber
Babies are our business...
and have been for over 50 years.
Gerber Products Company, Fremont, MI 49412

We've learned a lot about food because we care a lot about babies.

1980- Note the change in the wording of the slogan: Babies are our Business... and have been for over fifty years.

We helped nature make a better peach for Bobby.

Bobby is very particular about peaches. Like most babies, Bobby likes them best when they're smooth and sweet. So we gave Rutgers University a grant to develop just such a peach. The result was The Baby Gold Peach, Varieties #5, 6, 7, 8 and 9...specifically developed to reach maturity at one-week intervals so they could mature naturally on the tree. Since they grow sweet in the sun, "Baby Gold" peaches are naturally sweet...which makes Bobby's peaches more naturally sweet too. "Baby Gold" is just one of many varieties of peaches we use, and just one example of the Gerber commitment to prepare wholesome food for your baby. We're very particular about our baby food, because we're particularly fond of babies like Bobby.

Gerber

Babies are our business... and have been for over 50 years.
Gerber Products Company, Fremont, MI 49412

We've learned a lot about food because we care a lot about babies.

Family Circle March 1981.

BRIEF HISTORY OF GERBER PRODUCTS COMPANY

This article supplements the article titled "The Development of an Idea". It is a brief, concise account of the development of Gerber Products Company, its marketing plan, the standards by which it operated and grew, the challenges it faced along the way, its financial history and finally, the diversification of its product lines.

After modest beginnings with strained foods,(1) new products were often added to the line to remain a competitive leader. Baby cereals were added in 1932, eventually replacing "Pablum", an actual brand name that became a generic term. Junior foods were brought out in 1938, later teething biscuits, infant formulas, toddler meals and others.

Growth was not automatic and never easy. There were approximately 68 competitors in the baby food business between 1932 and 1935 alone. Gerber leads the only three survivors with about 70% of the market, followed by Heinz and Beech-Nut sharing the remainder. Along the way there have been troublesome challenges by competitors and the Federal Trade Commission about monopolizing the market, and in 1977 a pitched battle against an unwelcome takeover attempt by Anderson, Clayton and Co.

Gerber has always been aware that births plus "brand share" equals growth. Since babies grow up and move to table food, employees were reminded that they lost thousands of satisfied customers every day. The challenge was always to

(2)

reach the newborn replacements. From the 1940's through the 1960's, before commercial name lists were developed, Gerber recruited individuals from everywhere across the United States to copy and send in birth names and addresses from the local newspapers. The pay was small but worthwhile, and the names poured in, representing 80-85% of the babies born each year.

The front line for all of Gerber's marketing efforts, however, has always been the sales people calling on buyers at stores around the USA and beyond. In early years the salesmen traveled in fleet vehicles designed with the company name and logo.(2) In the 1980's the sales force totaled over 1000 people, with the majority of their time actually spent stocking the shelves in the stores, and keeping the display neat in front of the shoppers. They, and the competitors, always jockeyed for more shelf space for their brand to gain an advantage.

Another kind of sales force should also be mentioned, namely a second group of people who did only medical detailing. For years they called on pediatricians and physicians to explain and promote the nutritious and beneficial aspects of the products. They would leave literature and samples which the doctors could share with their patients.

(1)

199

Standards

(3)

In the end the product is what sells - obviously. Already in 1930 a nationally known dietitian was employed to develop and promote sound nutrition in baby foods.**(3)**The first objective was always to deliver top quality products to mothers, and nothing less would do. In-store follow up removed dents, torn labels and outdated cans from the displays with full reimbursement to the retailer. The most difficult product decision faced along the way was the conversion from 'tin' cans to glass jars. This was not only costly for new machines, but technically difficult to maintain a vacuum seal and avoid breakage and tampering. Also, the product color had to be the same for each variety regardless of where or when it was packed, so the food would look the same in the jars side by side in the stores.

To assure consistently high quality nutritious products took a great deal of effort by product developers, agricultural researchers, company field representatives and growers. Both employees and university researchers worked at length to develop the best food and crop varieties, growing areas and conditions, safe pest control and harvesting procedures. Again, these efforts were nationwide as manufacturing was spread out to five plants, partly to avoid disaster in case of crop failure in any one region. Stringent quality control procedures were maintained during and after production. (Oakland, California, 1943-1985; Niagara Falls, Ontario, 1947-1990; Rochester, New York, 1951-1980; plants in Asheville, North Carolina (1958) and Fort Smith, Arkansas (1962) are still in operation.)

Throughout its operation a main emphasis within the company was on the value and contribution of each employee as an individual.**(4)**Regardless of rank or type of job, management sincerely encouraged the best performance from each person: "Making our best better", it was called. For most people a strong camaraderie developed from knowing that the customers were well served and happy, demonstrated both by strong sales and earnings, and by a very positive public image, all as a result of teamwork throughout the company. Management encouraged quality, performance, and a high ethical standard in all dealings. Employees were satisfied when they did their part in reaching these goals.

Challenges:

All of the above is not to say that this was a company without problems. There were and are consumer complaints and inquiries to be dealt with. Consumer correspondents handle each situation promptly and personally, almost always to the satisfaction of the customer. Also, at times medical opinion has been divided over the adequacy of commercial foods or formulas, and these challenges had to be resolved. In the most recent compromise, Gerber is stating that "breast is best, but...".

Then, too, there have been a few employee strikes in the production plants, but not many.

And there have been the legal challenges mentioned earlier. But overall the reputation of the firm and its products remains held in high esteem by the public.

Financial:

The financial history of the company shows many lean years through the Great Depression of the 1930's until 1941. With small profits reinvested, the sale of preferred stock, and some cautious bank support the business developed. The first sales of common stock occurred in 1945, traded 'over-the-counter'. Gerber (GEB) was listed on the New York Stock Exchange on September 18, 1956.

Sales development at ten year intervals is shown below. Profits grew proportionately.

Year	$ Millions	Year	$Millions
1930	2.2	1970	237.9
1940	3.0	1980	602.0
1950	42.2	1990	1,136.4
1960	136.5	1993	1,269.5

International Market:

Expansion into the international market began as early as 1932 when Gerber contracted with Fine Foods of Canada Ltd. (later to be known as Green Giant of Canada) to manufacture baby foods under the Gerber label and "to use the Gerber trademarks and goodwill for Canda and all British possessions". * Because of duty regulations it was not practical to try to ship baby food over the border. Export food sales began in the 1950's and grew steadily in distribution into 75 countries. An international division was formed to oversee foreign sales and manufacturing. These efforts usually involved partners or licensees, and

they experienced ups and downs due to business and political reasons. Some of the major countries involved in the international market in the 1950's were Cuba, Venezuela, Australia, Mexico and South America. The 1960's added Japan, France, England, Puerto Rico and West Germany. In the 1970's South Korea, Italy, Greece, the Philipines, Russia, Egypt, and Iran were also added. In all Gerber expanded its distribution into 75 countries.

Diversification:

Eventually it could be seen that the U.S. food business could not sustain the growth rates of the past, and international growth was difficult. Strong cash flows permitted diversification into many other ventures starting in the 1960's. New products and services came to include life and health insurance, child care centers, children's toys, furniture and clothing lines, as well as can-making and trucking. These efforts, too, saw many slips and falls among a few successes, notably the very successful Gerber Life Insurance Company.

In 1994 a merger was completed with Sandoz of Switzerland.The company continues to be a strong leader in baby food and baby care products. Certain familiar aspects of the company have been affected by the change of ownership, but overall things appear to remain about the same. The future of Gerber Products Company, headquarted in Fremont , Michigan remains to be seen.

Matthew Okkema, Treasurer, Gerber Products Company, 1975-1991; Vice President and Treasurer 1991-1993.

Pictures for this article were made available through the courtesy of Gerber Products Company Archives; Sherrie Harris, Corporate Librarian.

(*Brooks, Sid. History of the Fremont Canning Company and Gerber Products Co.)

Is It Rubber or Vinyl ?
By Ed Mobley

An Overview

People know what they like and they like what they know. The more informed and knowledgeable a collector can become the better and more gratifying his/her collection will be. As one learns more about the chosen collection the information gathered adds to one's personal expertise in appraisal, selection and purchase.

Collector friends of mine have often proudly displayed their collections of vinyl dolls and animals I have designed as "Mobley Rubber Toys". Some catalogs I have examined, and toy / doll dealers I have visited, also mistakenly classify VINYL TOYS as rubber — which is often incorrect.

Serious collectors of items made of rubber and / or rubber-like vinyl material need to be aware of the characteristics of each product to be able to identify the objects correctly. Knowing the composition of these materials will lead to a better understanding of the materials and the process necessary to preserve them. The time period covered in this article is circa 1938 - 1973.

Prior to World War ll one of the first jointed RUBBER dolls was manufactured by the Sun Rubber Company of Barberton, Ohio. This "Sunbabe®" doll, a forerunner of the 1955 Sun Rubber 12 inch and 13 inch Gerber® baby dolls, was a fully-jointed baby doll with separately molded arms, legs, body and head which snap-locked naturally together. When rubber was designated a strategic war material, producers of rubber toys converted to defense production. At the end of WW ll (1945) U.S. industry quickly returned to producing consumer products of every description. This included dolls and children's playthings.

In the post-war period Sun Rubber and other rubber toy manufactures poured millions of dollars into retooling with expensive, heavy steam-jacketed molding presses which had been used so successfully to produce war materials. Unfortunately, these were quickly outmoded by the development of poly vinyl chloride (PVC) resin by B.F. Goodrich. This new product, BFG Geon®, was a finely ground light-colored granular material, which could be molded into any shape or configuration, and yield a tough, flexible rubber-like product in any color of the rainbow. When properly formulated with fillers, stabilizers, color, antioxidants and plasticizers, it became a creamy liquid which could be poured into a mold. A full cure was attained in a few minutes with less than 300° F. heat. No pressure or heavy mixing or complicated processing equipment was required.

A major revolution in the production of flexible rubber-like products had begun. PVC plastisol, or vinyl, was here to stay. The Polymer Age had begun! In the U.S. toy industry, high volume vinyl doll production became a reality by late 1951 and early 1952.

Getting Technical : Manufacturing in Rubber

To fully understand the aging process of rubber dolls and toys one needs to have a basic understanding of the processes used in the manufacturing of them. Molded rubber doll parts have a very poor shelf life! Every molded rubber part begins to oxidize with aging and may become boardy, brittle and distorted. Eventually, the older dolls can crumble and go to dust. Rare old rubber toys will disintegrate if not handled and stored very carefully. In 1946 most molded rubber toy and doll parts were made by compression molding using high temperatures, and heavy pressure on the mold cavity to accomplish the cure of the rubber compound. This accounts for the parting lines from the base of the neck, through the ears and across the head . This parting line will also appear along the sides of the body and arms and legs running from the joint across fingers and toes. This is evident in the bodies and limbs of the 12 inch and 13 inch Sun Rubber Gerber baby dolls. However, Sun Rubber did make a very few vinyl doll heads and toys in two piece molds in their earliest production of those toys. Evidence of this is the head and body of the 18 inch Gerber Baby dolls manufactured in 1955. Generally speaking, vinyl dolls will have no parting line on any molded parts.

Three methods were used in the manufacturing of rubber dolls and toys. Briefly, they are:

Method A. A solid chunk of uncured rubber stock was placed in a mold cavity. Heavy pressure and high temperature forced the rubber to conform to the mold. Excess rubber (flash) was squeezed out the parting line and buffed off after curing. Examples are solid rubber toy parts or a rubber mallet head.

Method B. Core molded rubber doll parts had a steel core designed to take up most of the empty space between the top and bottom of the mold cavity. A thin sheet of uncured rubber was placed in the lower half of the mold. Next, the steel core was put in place and then another thin sheet of rubber was placed on top. Then the mold was closed under great pressure and heat. After the part was cured the molds were opened. The core would remain on the bottom half of the mold. Air pressure was used to removed the cured rubber molded part off the core. This is how the original Sunbabe® rubber doll was made.

Method C. Early hollow dolls were made by "blowing " uncured rubber against the top and bottom mold halfs. This involved thin sheets of especially compounded rubber which was soft and spongy. Sodium bicarbonate placed inside this "biscuit" created the internal pressure to force the uncured rubber to conform to the two piece compression mold. Millions of toys were made by Sun Rubber and other toy manufacturers using this method.

There were two other types of rubber toys made during my life in the toy design business:

Method A. Latex toys were produced by "dipping" a metal form into tanks of liquid latex. The form was first coated with a solution to cause the raw latex to gel. Once the form acquired a thin layer of latex it was dipped into second tank to set the rubber film. Toys were decorated while still on the form and cured in an oven The simplest example is the rubber balloon.

Method B. A very innovative procedure was used by Rempel Mfg. of Akron, Ohio. Toys were "roto-molded" in plaster of Paris molds. Rempel's latex compounds were formulated with fillers to give more rigidity. Excess water was evacuated through the porous wall of the plaster. Molds were replaced as they became pitted from use. These toys were highly creative in design and beautifully decorated. However, they did not age well and few are found today. Those that remain would be very collectible.

Manufacturing in Vinyl

Method A.The process called Slush Molding used electro-formed mold cavities made of copper. The doll heads, bodies, arms and legs were designed with an opening at one end of the mold which was filled with uncured plastisol (vinyl) . The outside surface was heated until a thin wall of vinyl was gelled on the inner wall of the mold and then excess liquid vinyl was slushed out to be used in the next mold. The mold then went into an oven, or into heated liquid, to cure. After cooling to 120° F the doll part could be easily stripped out of the warm copper mold. This left no visual parting lines.

Method B. Mass production of molded vinyl toys and dolls were mostly produced by the Rotational Molding method. The new varieties of machines available to toy manufactures nearly all used the electroformed molds to duplicate their products. Only a few used two-piece molds of thin walled cast aluminum.

Each machine had multiple mold cavities (12-18-24) mounted in a frame usually called a spider. Each mold had a mechanical closure. Metered pumps dispensed the exact amount of liquid plastisol into each cavity. The caps were closed and the entire "spider" of molds was moved into the oven chamber for heat curing. The machine continued to rotate the "spider" to spread an even wall of vinyl as it gelled and cured. Water and/or air was used during the cooling cycle.Then the molds were mechanically opened and stripped out using vacuum tubes to deflate the very flexible and still warm part. Properly cured these pieces have no distortion though severely stretched in the process. There is no flash (extra material) or parting lines on any part .

Collecting and Care of Rubber and Vinyl toys.

Sun Rubber dominated the rubber toy industry for many years. Millions of toys were made but few remain today. Rubber toys contain sulfur, and as was explained earlier will begin to oxidize within months after curing. This shows up as a "bloom" on the surface . This fine dust can be washed off, helping to preserve the toy.However, eventually all rubber toys will harden and deteriorate. Those toys from Sun still in collections must be stored away from UV exposure and handled with extreme care. Most still available will be found at sales in Ohio, Michigan and Indiana. In good condition they are very valuable.

Unlike toys made of rubber vinyl toys are nearly indestructible, and will last a long time if properly cared for. In my personal collection of vinyl dolls and animals are parts made in 1949 which are still in mint condition. Aging characteristics of molded vinyl toys or dolls include :

1. When exposed to sunlight for extended periods they will turn dark in color. (Avoid excess UV exposure to your collectibles).

2. In the first ten years they may exude uncured plasticizer to the surface, which leaves a greasy feel. (Wash off with mild soap and water). Do not store your collection on varnished or lacquered shelves, as the plasticizer can attack the painted surface.

3. As these toys age beyond ten years, they may shrink slightly in size when most of the plasticizers have been lost. This shrinkage is uniform throughout the part and details become even sharper to the eye.

4. At this time the toy is slightly less flexible than when it was first molded, but it is not stiff and boardy.

5. Distortion can occur if the toy has been stored out of

shape against other items. Most distortion can be removed by immersing the part in a sink of hot water (or a light tumble in your laundry dryer !). Vinyl has a memory, so that when exposed to heat the molded part returns to to its original contours. After distortion is removed , use cold water to "fix" the shape you have achieved with heat. It will remain that way.

6. Badly soiled and dirty vinyl toys are cleaned with hot water and a mild soap unless grit is embedded in the surface. (Avoid excess rubbing pressure on doll faces when cleaning, because the paint may wash off in the process.)

7. Store your vinyl collections in clean polyethylene bags and on a bed of acid-free tissue or soft cloth to avoid distortion in storage.

In Conclusion:

The sudden creation of many different vinyl molding firms in the 1950-60 era resulted in hundreds of different dolls, animals and syndicated characters for your present collecting interests. I have personally created models in various sizes, positions and costumes of important Walt Disney and Hanna & Barbera characters to establish a special collection niche — all by myself! This is only the tip of the iceberg. There are many hundreds of designs made by others over the years. Your collecting possibilities are very wide indeed!

These products were distributed in all major chain stores of the day and could now be found in yard sales or flea markets in any state in the U.S. — and in much of Canada. Some of these were made for only a limited period, so they could be very scarce by now.

Good luck in your search! Enjoy collecting something that once made children smile and created love that lasts forever.

Background information on Ed Mobley

Ed was a full scholarship student at the Cleveland School of Art when Japan bombed Pearl Harbor. When that happened he thought his dreams of becoming a painter and illustrator were over. By the next autumn he was in the Mojave Desert training with the 6th Armored Division. From that time until January, 1946, his Army duties included: Topographer for the Combat Command of Sixth Armored— Japanese Language School—Traffic Analyst on inter-

cepted Japanese radio traffic at Vint Hill Farms— and routine duties with the Counter Intelligence Corps.

After his discharge from the Army Ed went to work as an apprentice in the Art and Design department of Sun Rubber in Barberton, Oh. At that time Sun Rubber was the largest and most successful rubber toy and doll company in the world. " That extreme good fortune put me inside one of the most secret inner-sanctums of product development then existing for dolls and toys made of rubber. I became Director of Art and Design for Sun in 1953, and in early 1958 resigned to establish my own free-lance Industrial Design business."

Working out of his independent studio in his home in rural N.E. Ohio (Akron area) Ed's adult life became totally involved with creation and development of toys, dolls and playthings, including package designs for these products. In 1973 he moved away from creative toy design work to National Marketing Director of other rubber products until retirement in May, 1995. In retirement he enjoys being an artist, designer, painter, marketing man, gem cutter, rockhound —-and collector.

" Since I was personally present in those meetings at Fremont, Michigan with Dan Gerber and TW Smith (President of Sun Rubber) to discuss the development of the first "Gerber Baby" rubber doll—- and remained at Sun during the birth and product life of the Baby Doll — I am pleased to be asked to contribute to this work by Joan Stryker Grubaugh".

ABOUT THE AUTHOR

Joan was born in Fremont, Michigan, at Gerber Memorial Hospital, on January 13, 1930. She was the second daughter of Dr. Oscar Stryker, who practiced medicine in Fremont from 1929 to 1947. Joan attended Fremont Public Schools from kindergarten through ninth grade when she left Fremont to attend Milwaukee Downer Seminary in Milwaukee, Wisconsin.She graduated from there in 1948 and subsequently went on to earn her BS degree from Northwestern University in 1952, a MA degree from Rockford College, Illinois in 1976, and her Ed.D. degree from Arizona State University in 1983. Joan is married to Beryl Grubaugh and has two married daughters, a married son, and six grand children. Since retiring from a teaching career she and her husband have moved from Arizona back to Ohio to live in their century old, newly- remolded Grubaugh family farm home.

Joan's fondest memories are of her growing-up years in Fremont. She recalls the times she and her sister (who has been collecting Gerber baby dolls for a long time), joined other classmates weeding in the onion and carrot fields of the farmers who grew vegetables for Gerbers. It was hot, hard work, even for a kid, but every one was doing it. (On your hands and knees you straddled one row and weeded that row and the one on either side of it. She remembers the rows as being at least a mile long ! You were paid by the number of rows you weeded.) She much preferred to stay at her family's cottage on Fremont Lake to swim, fish or go boating. When school started again in the Fall, and the family moved back to town, the work for the Gerber farmers was to pick apples, pears, and peaches. That was more fun and better pay than onions and carrots.

Joan recalls the benefits of growing up in a small town, the innocence of growing up in an age before TV, a time when your moral standards and your outlook on life came from your family, your church, your school, and your community. She recalls the pride one had of living in a small town where many of the town people and the surrounding farming community worked in or for the ever-growing, nationally- known Gerber Baby Food Company. Joan still answers the age old question asked by new acquaintances- "and where did you come from originally?" The answer: "Fremont, Michigan"—quickly followed by, "the home of Gerber Baby Food" — which, then, always brings a look of recognition.

Bibliography

Brooks, Sid. *The History of Fremont Canning Co. and Gerber Products Company.* Fremont, Michigan: Gerber Products Company, 1986.

Fifty Years of Caring. Fremont, Michigan: Gerber Products Company, 1978.

The Story of an Idea. Fremont, Michigan: Gerber Products Company, 1953.

Perkins, Myla. *Black Dolls, Identification and Values: 1820-1991.* 1993. Page 145.

Perkins, Myla. *Black Dolls, Identification and Value Guide, Book 2.* 1995. Collection of African American History, Detroit. Page, 186.

Robinson, Joleen Ashman and Kay F. Sellers. *Advertising Dolls: Identification and Value Guide.* Paducah Ky : Collector Books, April, 1992, Pgs.155-159.

Smith, Pat. *Doll Values, Antique to Modern, 11th Edition.* Paducah, Ky.: Collector Books, 1995. Page 215.

Smith, Pat. *Modern Collector's Dolls- Identification and Value Guide- Seventh Series,* Paducah, Ky.: Collector Books, 1995. P.134.

Smith, Pat. *Modern Collector's Dolls- Price Update- 1995 Revised Values.* Paducah, Ky.: Collector Books, 1995. P. 38.

Strahlendorf, Evelyn. *The Charleston Price Guide to Canadian Dolls, First Edition.* 15 Birch Ave., Toronto, Canada, M4V 1E1: The Charleston Press, 1990. P.37.

Articles , Pamphlets and Press Releases

Atlanta Novelty, A Division of Gerber Products Company catalog, 1981.

Gerber Dolls
Gerber Products Company/ Corporate Library and Archives, September 17, 1981.

Gerber News, 1980-1990.

Gerber® Toy Line Catalog, 1969.

Kurtz, Karen B. *Cuddly Gerber Baby Dolls,* <u>Doll World</u>, April, 1995. Pgs. 34-36.

Sun Rubber Co. Catalog, 1955

Teague, Phyllis E. *That Gorgeous Gerber Baby.* <u>National Doll World Christmas Annual</u>, 1981. The House of White Birches, Inc., Seabrook N.H. 03874. Pgs. 28-30.

Wank, Marty and Audrey. *Treasure Trove,* Late Summer, 1980. Manhasset, N.Y. 11030.

Wank, Marty and Audrey. *Treasure Trove,* Spring, 1981. Manhasset, N. Y. 11030.

Wolfe, Alma. *Gerber Baby Doll- The Family Tree.* <u>Doll Reader</u>, April / May 1980. P.38.
.
Wolfe, Alma. *Addenda, Gerber Baby Doll... The Family Tree.* <u>Doll Reader</u>, April./.May, 1981. P.118.

Collector's Photo Index and Price Guide to the Gerber® Baby–The World's Best Known Baby

PART 1 GERBER BABY DOLLS	PRICE

Plates 1-2

1936 8 inch Cloth Girl Premium $400.00*

1936 8 Inch Cloth Girl Doll in Original Packageing . . . . $500.00+

Plates 3-4

1936 8 inch Cloth Boy Premium $400.00*

1936 8 inch Cloth Boy Doll in Original Packageing . . . . $500.00+

Sun Rubber Company 1955-1958

Plates 5-7

12 inch Premium— with Accessories $140.00

12 inch Doll Nude or Redressed . . . . $50.00-$75

Plates 8-9

12 inch Sunruco, Canada— Premium 1955—No Accessories. . . . . $100.-$125.

Comparison of Sun Rubber and Sunruco dolls

Gerber Baby Doll Sunruco Head on Sun Rubber Body- Nude or Redressed . . . .$50.-$75.

Plate 10

12 inch The Gerber Baby Formula Set, Retail . . . . $225.00 +

Plate11

12 inch Sun Rubber Retail Doll in Original Outfit $125.00

Plate 12

13 inch The Gerber Baby Formula Set, Retail . . . . $250.00 +

Plate 13

Head of 13 inch Sun Rubber doll . . . .

Plate 14

18 inch The Gerber Baby Formula Set, Retail . . . . $275.00 +

Plate 15

Undressed 18 inch Sun Rubber doll— or Redressed $100.00

Plate 16

18 inch Sun Rubber Doll Dressed in Original Gown $175.00

Plate 17

18 inch Sun Rubber Doll Dressed in Original Playsuit and Bib $175.00

Arrow Rubber and Plastic Co. 1965

Plates 18 - 20

14 inch Premium in Original Diaper and Bib, Box . . . . $75.00-$125.00

14 inch Premium Undressed or Redressed. . . . . $40.-$60.

Amsco - A Milton Bradley Company, 1972-1973

Plate 21

10 inch Premium / Black in Original Outfit $60.00*; $150.00**

Black Nude or Redressed Body . . . . $60.-$100.

Plate 22

10 inch Premium / White in Original Outfit $50.00

White Nude or Redressed Body . . . . $35.-$40.

Plates 23-24

Comparison of 10 inch Premium and Retail Dolls Hair Lines

Plates 25-26

Comparison of 10 inch Premium & Retail Dolls Eyes, Face, Mouth and Feet

Plates 27-28

Comparison of 10 inch Premium and Retail Dolls Back Marking

Photo Index and Price Guide (continued)

Photo Index and Price Guide (continued)

Photo Index and Price Guide (continued)

Plate 81
    17 inch Mama Voice, Pink Checked Body Suit, Extra Outfit, Spoon/Black $100.00
Plate 82-83
    Undressed Wet and Drink Doll to Show Opening for Water Release $45.00
Plate 84
    17 inch Drink and Wet in Trunk with Accessories/ Black $110.00
Plate 85
    17 inch Drink and Wet / in Trunk with Accessories / White $110.00

1981

Plates 86-87
    Undressed, Flesh Tones, Plain Bodies of 12 inch Dolls $30.00
Plate 88
    12 inch Collector Doll in Christening Gown /White in Basket. $100.00
Plate 89
    12 inch Collector Doll in Christening Gown / Black in Basket $100.00
Plate 91
    12 inch Miss Pinafore, with Accessories/Black $100.00
Plate 92
    12 inch Miss Pinafore with Accessories/ White. $100.00
Plate 90
    Two Little Miss Pinafores without Accessories. $75.00
Plate 93-94
    Undressed 12 inch Drink and Wet Dolls $35.00
Plate 95
    12 inch Drink and Wet /Black in Basket with Accessories (JC Penneys) $100.00
Plate 96
    12 inch Drink and Wet / White in Basket with Accessories (JC Penneys) $100.00
Plates 97-98
    Undressed Bodies of 12 inch Cries Mama Dolls. $45.00
Plate 99
    12 inch Cries Mama / Black in Basket with Accessories $95.00
Plate 100
    12 inch Cries Mama / White in Basket with Accessories $95.00
Plate 101
    Cries Mama Dressed in her Sunday Best! $75.00
Plate 102
    12 inch Cries Mama in Baby Carrier, 2 Extra Outfits, Toy/ White $110.00
Plate 103
    12 inch Cries Mama in Baby Carrier, 2 Extra outfits, Toy/ Black $110.00

1985

Plate 104-105
    Nude Bodies of 12 inch All Vinyl Dolls $25.00
Plate 106
    12 inch Vinyl, Foam Filled in Pink Tub with Accessories, Premium / Black $95.00
Plate 107
    12 inch Vinyl, Foam Filled in Pink Tub with Accessories, Premium/White $95.00
Plate 108
    Above Dolls Dressed in Their Packaged Dresses $35.00

Photo Index and Price Guide (continued)

Plate 109
 12 inch Vinyl, Foam Filled in Blue Tub with Accessories, Premium/ White $95.00
Plate 110
 12 inch Vinyl, Foam Filled in Blue Tub with Accessories, Premium/ Black $95.00
Plate 111-112
 17 inch Vinyl, Foam Filled in Pink Tub with Accessories, Premium/White $100.00
Plate 113
 17 inch Vinyl, Foam Filled in Pink Tub with Accessories, Premium/Black. $100.00
Plate 114
 17 inch Vinyl, Foam Filled in Blue Tub with Accessories, Premium/Black. $100.00
Plate 115
 17 inch Vinyl, Foam Filled in Blue Tub with Accessories, Premium/White $100.00
Plate 116
 All Vinyl Dolls with Some Accessories not Boxed. $45.00
Plate 117
 12 inch Vinyl, Foam Filled Retail Dolls with Accessories $45.00

1984

Plate 118
 White Plush Musical Dolls, Black/White $75.00
Plate 119
 Back View Showing Wind-up Key Location.
Plate 120
 Pink Plush Musical Doll in Original Box $95.00

Limited Edition Porcelain

Plate 121
 1981 14 inch Porcelain / (White) Cloth $350.00
Plate 122
 1981 14 inch Porcelain / Cloth (Alternate Material in Dress) $350.00
Plate 123
 1982 12 inch Porcelain / (Pink) Cloth $350.00
Plate 124
 A Close-up View of the Beautiful Face of the 1982 Porcelain Gerber Baby Doll
Plate 125
 1983 10 inch Porcelain / Cloth Boy Twin doll. . . . . $350 ea.
Plate 126
 1983 10 inch Porcelain / Cloth Girl Twin doll . . . . $350 ea.

Lucky Ltd. 1989-1992

Plate 127
 6 inch- White $15.00
 6 inch-Black $15.00
Plates 128-129
 Undressed Bodies of 6 inch dolls. $5.00
Plate 130
 6 inch Vinyl Gerber Birthday Baby Twins ,White $40.00
Plate 131
 11 inch Drink and Wet - Black/ White with Accessories $45.00
Plate 132
 11 inch Drink and Wet- White / Black in Original Outfit without Accessories $25.00
Plate 133
 11 inch Drink and Wet in Playsuit and Accessories- Black/White. $45.00

Photo Index and Price Guide (continued)

Plate 134
　　Plate Showing Lucky Logo on Vinyl Body- Undressed doll $20.00
Plate 135-136
　　Undressed Soft Body of 14 inch Lucky Doll $20.00
Plate 137
　　Baby Doll Traveler Set- White Doll in Pink $45.00
Plate 138
　　Gerber Baby Gift Set. $45.00
Plate 139
　　Soft Body Doll in Original Clothes with Accessories $45.00
Plates 140-141
　　Undressed Bodies of 16 inch Soft Body Lucky Dolls $25.00
Plates 142-43
　　16 inch - Black in Original Dress $40.00
　　16 inch - White in Original Dress $40.00
Plates 144-145
　　Undressed Bodies of 21 inch Lucky doll $30.00
Plate 146
　　21 inch Doll in Original Outfit $55.00

Toy Biz, Inc. 1994-1996

1994

Plate 147
　　15 inch Potty Time Baby / Black. $25.00
　　15 inch Potty Time Baby / White. $25.00
Plate 148
　　Undressed Form $10.00
Plate 149
　　15 inch Tub Time / Black $25.00
　　15 inch Tub Time / White. $25.00
Plate 150
　　Undressed form $10.00
Plate 151
　　15 inch Loving Tears Baby / Black $25.00
　　15 inch Loving Tears Baby / White. $25.00
Plate 152
　　Undressed Form $10.00
Plate 153
　　15 inch Feel Better Baby / Black. $25.00
　　15 inch Feel Better Baby / White $25.00
Plate 154
　　15 inch Food Time Baby / Black. $25.00
　　15 inch Food Time Baby / White. $25.00
Plate 155
　　15 inch Food and Playtime Baby / White $25.00
Plate 156
　　14 inch Talking Baby / White Boy $40.00
　　14 inch Talking Baby / White Girl. $40.00
Plate 157
　　14 inch Talking Baby / Black Boy $40.00
　　14 inch Talking Baby / Black Girl $40.00

Photo Index and Price Guide (continued)

Plate 158
    14 inch Talking Baby / Hispanic Boy $40.00
    14 inch Talking Baby / Hispanic Girl $40.00
Plate 159
    Computer Box Location
Plate 160
    12 inch Play Time Baby $22.00
Plate 161
    The Gerber First Sounds Baby Doll $25.00
Plate 162
    Opening for Batteries
Plate 163
    13 inch Newborn Baby / Black $25.00
    13 inch Newborn Baby / White $25.00
Plate 164
    13 inch Lullaby Baby / Black $25.00
    13 inch Lullaby Baby / White- $25.00
Plate 165
    Computer Box Opening . . . .
Plate 166
    13 inch Twins / White $25.00
Plate 167
    17 inch Collector Doll / Black $50.00
    17 inch Collector Doll / White $50.00
    17 inch Collector Doll / Hispanic $50.00

1996

Plates 168-169
    8 inch Fruit Babies / Black $15.00
    8 inch Fruit Babies / White $15.00
Plate 170
    14 inch A.B.C.Talking Doll $40.00
Plate 170 A
    Baby Care Set $25.00
Plate 176
    Lucky 9" Vinyl on Generic Body $15.00
Plate 182
    14" All Porcelain Look-alike $185.00
Plate 183
    14" All Porcelain Look-alike $175.00
Plate 187
    9" All Porcelain Look-alike $95.00
Plate 188
    14" All Porcelain Look-alike $175.00

* Pat Smith "Doll Values, Antique to Modern", 1995.

*** Myla Perkins. Black Dolls, Identification and Value Guide", 1995.

Photo Index and Price Guide (continued)

PART 2 - GERBER COLLECTIBLES

Baby Care/ Wear
Plate 1
SH.H.HH ! Baby's Asleep Sign - Die Cut,1972 . . . . $14.00
SH.HH.H ! Baby's Asleep Sign From the 40's-50's $12.00
SH.HH.H ! Sign, Bottom Row,1954 . . . . $10.00
Plate 2
Back Side of Above Signs Showing Gerber Line of Baby Foods
Plate 3
Gerber Disposal Wash Cloths.1970's. $8.00
Plate 4
Gerber Baby Travel Kit. 1988 . . . . $10.00
Plates 5-6
Baby Thermometer Designed for Baby's Bath. 1938- Premium $75.00
Plate 7
Gerber Babywear Department Store Sign, 1965 . . . . $70.00
Plate 8
Gerber Babywear Gift Set,1980 . . . . $20.00
Plate 9
Gerber Infant Care Products Kit, 1980. . . . . $10.00
Plate 10
Baby Fever Thermometer, 1990 . . . . $4.00
Plate 11
Fire Alert Decal, 1990 . . . . $2.00
Refrigerator Magnet, 1990. . . . . $6.00
Jar Opener, 1990 . . . . $3.50

Baby Feeding Time
Plate 12
Blue Plastic Baby Bottles Shaped Like a Penguin or Kitten, 1970's. $10.00
Plate 13
Heart Decorated Plastic Baby Bottle, 1990 . . . . $3.00
Heart Decorated Graduate Drinking Cup, 1990. . . . . $3.00
Plate 14
Silk Screened Tumblers, 1950's. $13.50
Plate 15
Embossed Plastic Tumblers, 1971. . . . . $3.00
Plate 16
Cereal Bowl and Tumbler Set. Premium Offer 1971 . . . . $9.00
Plate 17
Two Handle Drinking Cup, 1990 . . . . $3.00
Plate 18
Gift set of 24 Jars of Gerber Baby Food, 1940's $125.00
Plate 19
Gerber Baby Can Cover, 1955. . . . . $22.00
Plate 20-Premiums
Winthrop Baby Head Shaped, SP Spoon, 4 1/4", Premiums '41, '46-'56 . . . . $30.00
Winthrop Silverplate Educator Spoon, 4 1/2", 1957-1972. . . . . $15.00
Winthrop Silverplate Spoons, 5 1/2", 1957-1972 . . . . $12.00
Plate 21- Premiums
Oneida Silverplate Spoon , 5 1/2 ". Marked Wm. Rogers.1972, Rare $20.00
Oneida Educator Spoons, Stainless Steel, 4 1/2', 1972-1996 . . . . $8.00

Photo Index and Price Guide (continued)

Photo Index and Price Guide (continued)

Plate 38
    Heavy Weight Sweatshirt, 1990 . . . . $20.00
    Graduate Sweatshirt, 1990 . . . . $15.00
Plate 39
    T Shirt with Gerber Baby and Blue Trim $18.00
Plate 40
    Toddler T Shirt with the words: World's Best Known Baby, 1982 . . . . $18.00
Plate 41
    White Golf Sweater, 1990's $35.00
    Workers Square Scarf, 1950's $38.00
Plate 118
    Baseball Cap, Cornacopia Farms, Late 70's $8.00
Plate 42
    Adult T Shirt, 1978 . . . . $10.00
    Child's T Shirt, 1978 . . . . $10.00
Plate 43
    T Shirt with all Over Print of Gerber Baby Face, 1990's $8.00
    Gerber Graduate T Shirt, 1990 . . . . $8.00
Plate 44
    Knitted Shoe Mittens, 1984 . . . . $13.00
Plate 45
    Convenient Travel Kit, 1986 . . . . $12.00
Plate 46
    Roll Up T Shirts, 1990's $8.00

Gerber Corporate ID Items

  Plate 47
    Gerber Metal License Plate, 1981 . . . . $14.00
Plate 48
    Swiss Army Knife, 1986 . . . . $18.00
    Mag-Lite $13.00
    Brass Key Chain, 1990's $7.00
Plate 49
    Square Key Tag with Gerber Baby Face, 1990's. $5.00
    Graduates Key Chain, 1990's $5.00
    Ice Scraper, 1990's $5.00
    Flashlight Key Tag, 1990's. $5.00
    Luggage Tag, 1990's $5.00
Plate 50
    Sun Visor $15.00
Plate 51
    Clippers and Knife in Case, 1980's $5.00
    Shoe Shine Applicator in Case, 1975. . . . . $5.00
    Emery board $2.00
    Toothbrush Holder $2.00
    Rubber Jar Opener. $2.00
    Peep-through Layout Viewer, 1985 . . . . $25.00
    Band Aid Dispenser, 1977 . . . . $5.00
    Plastic Magnifying Glass. $3.00
    Funnel $2.00
Plate 52
    Gold Disk-Shaped Key Chain with Shield $15.00
    Gold Key-Shaped Key Chain with Blue Shield. $15.00

Photo Index and Price Guide (continued)

Gerber Graduate Key Chain $5.00
Plate 53
Gerber Baby Head Magnet, Current $6.00
Gerber® Toyline Magnet, Mid 80's $6.00
Gerber Baby Food Jar Magnet, Late 70's $6.00
Plate 54
Grill Scrapper, 1980's $4.00
Plate 55
Note pads with Gerber Baby Face, 1990's $4.00
Double Deck Playing Cards with Gerber Baby Face, 1990's $8.00
Zippy Letter Opener with Gerber Baby Face, 1990's $4.00
Plate 56
20 Wooden Match Boxes with Corporate Logos in Plastic Case, 1985 . . . . $25.00
Plate 57
Brass Coasters in Oak Holder, 1990's $30.00
Plate 58
Footed Covered Glass Candy Jar with Etched Gerber Baby Face $25.00
Plate 59
Gerber Baby Ladies Watch, 1970's $35.00
Plate 60
Book Matches, 1970's $6.00
Plate 61
Silver Money Clip, Gold Medallion, 'G' and Gerber Baby Head $15.00
Gold Money Clip with Gerber Baby Head Medallion and Diamond $18.00
Swiss Army Knife $18.00
Silver Money Clip with Gerber and Baby Head Screened in Blue $15.00
Gold Clip with Medallion, 'G' and Gerber Baby Head in Blue, 1980's $15.00
Plate 62
Clip Light, Gerber and Baby Face, 1986 . . . . $5.00
Dual Purpose Lighted Key Ring, 1985 . . . . $5.00
Night Light, late 1980's $8.00
Pen Light, 1980 . . . . $10.00

Gerber Life Insurance Co
Plate 63
Golf Umbrella,1990 . . . . $35.00
Cap, 1990 . . . . $8.00
Duffle Bag, 1990 . . . . $10.00
Calculator, 1980's $10.00
Jewelry, Pins
Plate 64
Gerber Graduate Lapel Pin, 1990's $4.00
Blue Lapel Pin with Gerber in Gold, 1990's $4.00
Gold Lapel Pin with Gerber Baby Face, 1990's $4.00
Plate 65
Quartz Watch, 1990's $30.00
Plate 66
Solid Pewter Pendant, 1979 . . . . $25.00
Plate 67
Gerber Baby Stick Pin, 1978 . . . . $45.00
Plate 68
Spoon Ring, 1978 . . . . $14.00

Photo Index and Price Guide (continued)

Plate 69
- Charm Bracelet $18.00
- Bronze Plated Belt Buckle, 1976 Premium. $35.00
- Gerber Baby Face Bronze Charm, 1960's - 1980's $75.00
- Gold Watch Bands, 1971 . . . . $22.00

Plate 70
- Silver Tie Clip with Gerber Baby and Script in Blue. $9.00
- Silver and Blue Gerber Baby Tie Tack $9.00
- Gold Plated Gerber Baby Head Tie Tack $9.00
- White Tie Tack with Gerber Baby Head in Blue $9.00
- Congratulations Card with #1 Tie Tack, 1988 . . . . $9.00
- Gerber 3rd Foods Tie Tack, 1980's. $9.00

Plate 71
- "I Have Visited The Gerber Baby" Lapel Pin, 3 1/4", 1941 . . . . $18.00
- "I Have Visited The Gerber Baby" Lapel Pin, 1 3/8", 1946. . . . . $18.00
- Gerber Baby Lapel Pin, Blue on White, 2 1/4" $8.00
- Gerber Graduate Pin, 1989. . . . . $5.00
- Gerber Super Service Pin, 1990 . . . . $5.00
- VP Identification Pin, 1986 . . . . $5.00
- Gerber Baby Lapel Pin, White on Dark Blue, 2 1/2". $18.00
- Gerber Baby 25th Anniversary Lapel Pin, 1 3/8", 1958 . . . . $22.00
- Gerber Baby Lapel Pin with Flag which Reads" Old Fashion Days/ Fremont, Mich." $40.00

Mugs, Drinking Glasses

Plates 72-73
- Plastic Mug with "Modilac', 1960-1970. . . . . $8.00

Plate 74
- Travel Mug with Lid and Special Base, 1990's. $6.00
- Can Cooler, 1990's $6.00

Plate 75
- Insulated White Mug, 1988. . . . . $6.00

Plate 76-77
- Ceramic Mug with Baby Bottle and "Gerber baby formula/with iron/etc. Late 80's. $10.00

Plate 78
- White Gerber Baby Mug with "Safety and Quality" etc. ,1987 . . . . $10.00

Plates 79-80
- Gerber Baby Mugs with Safety Slogans Screened on Reverse Side $10.00

Plate 81
- I'm A Gerber Bad Guy (Buck-A-Day) Mug,1984. . . . . $10.00

Plate 82
- "Medial Services" Mug. $10.00
- Stone ware Coffee Mug, 1988 . . . . $10.00

Plates 83-84
- Modilac Mug, 1970 . . . . $14.00
- "Dollars for Ideas" Mug $10.00
- Gerber Baby Mug with 3 Dancing Cans on the Reverse Side $10.00

Plate 85
- Gerber Baby Visitor's Center Opening Mug, 1990. . . . . $14.00

Plate 86
- White Grabber Mug with Gerber Baby Face in Blue,1984 . . . . $7.00
- Blue Grabber Mug with No Spill Lid and"Gerber". $7.00

Plate 87
- Insulated Beverage Mug with Lid, 1988. . . . . $7.00

Photo Index and Price Guide (continued)

Photo Index and Price Guide (continued)

Gerber Family News Release Folder. $10.00

Pens, Pencils and Desk Item
Plate 106- 1990's
Bic Executive Metal Point Pen, Message Call 1-800-4- Gerber. $1.50
Bic Clic Stick- with Special Message. $1.50
Highlighter Pen with Special Message $1.50
Wood Pencils feature Gerber Special message $1.50
Plate 107
Baby Bath Thermometer, 1930's. $75.00
Acrylic Paper Weight with Timer and Miniature Gerber Cereal Box, 1960's $25.00
Pencil Clips, 1930's. $9.00
Plate 108
Jumbo Ball Pen $6.00
Corporate Pens and Pencils from the 1980's and 1990's. $4.00
Plate 109
Cross Pen and Pencil Set, 1988. . . . . $50.00
Wood Paper Dispenser, 1989
Letter Opener in Case, 1970's. $14.00
Salesmen's Leather Record and/or Notebooks. $20.00
Plate 110
Metal 13" Ruler, 1960 . . . . $14.00
Metal 12" Ruler, 1959. . . . . $14.00
Folding Ruler $6.00
6" Plastic Ruler, 1950's. $5.00
Plate 111
Digital Clock Card Holder, 1985 . . . . $10.00
Paper Clip Dispenser, 1978 . . . . $4.00
Wood Grain Desk Organizer, 1989 . . . . $8.00
Digital Clock Card Holder, 1989 . . . . $11.00
Ball Pen Holder, 1972. . . . . $11.00
Plastic Card Holder, 1985 . . . . $6.00
Gold Metal Card Carrier, 1985 . . . . $28.00

Production and Sales
Plate 112
Ambassador Club Coupons and Pin $10.00
Gerber Travel Guide. $11.00
Gerber Drivers Manual $11.00
Salesmen's Food Coupon $5.00
Gerber News, Early Editions. $10.00
Plate 113
Salesmen's Calculators from the 1990's $5.00
Salesmen Directories from the 1980's and 1990's. $3.00
Plate 114
Grotape, 1969. . . . . $35.00
Gerber Baby Round White Tape $15.00
Federal Credit Union Tape $12.00
Gerber Baby Round Blue Tape $15.00
Plate 115
Gerber Baby Round Red and White Tape. $18.00
Plate 116

Photo Index and Price Guide (continued)

Cafeteria Tray, 1950's $40.00
Production Line Worker's Cap, 1940's $9.00
Plate 117
Box Top Cutter with *Babies are our business ...our only business*, 1940's $1.50
Box Top Cutter *Babies are our business....* $1.50
Paper Cutter with Gerber Employees Fed. Credit Union $1.50
Paper Cutter with Administrative Network.............................. $1.50
Scrapper Knife Gerber/ *Babies are our business etc.*, 1940's $10.00
Plate 118
Plastic Worker's Apron, 1930-1940's.................................. $10.00
Frisbee with Baby Face and Safety Slogan, Mid 80's.................... $7.00

Special Events
Plate 119
Gerber Baby Paper Stick-On Decal, 1970's $3.00
Fifty Years of Caring Cloth Patch, 1978 .... $6.00
Gerber Baby Cloth Sensitive Patches, 1981 .... $6.00
Plate 120
1990 Gerber Golf Open Etched Glass Pitcher $18.00
1989 Gerber Golf Open Hi Ball Etched Glass........................... $8.00
Gerber Baby Etched Glass Tumbler $8.00
Plate 121
50th Anniversary Bottle with Spoon and Coupon, 1978 .... $14.00
Gerber Baby Food Bottle from Asheville, NC Plant, 1958 .... $22.00
Plate 122
Six Pack Molded Plastic Cooler, 1991................................. $9.00
Plate 123
Styrofoam Can Holder, Gerber Open, 1982 .... $4.00
Plate 124
Gerber Baby Etched Crystal Bell, Late 1980's $95.00
Plate 125
Stork Club Tote Bag from 1978 Anniversary Celebration with Invitation $75.00
Plate 126
Invitation to 1978 Stork Club Celebration. $5.00
Plate 127
Bronze Gerber Baby Coin in Acrylic Paper Weight, 1978 .... $45.00
Bronze Gerber Baby Paper Weight, 1978 .... $45.00
Bronze Gerber Billion Dollar Club Weight, !989 .... $30.00
Plate 128
Gerber Baby Plastic Tote Bag, "50 Years of Caring", 1978............. $3.00
Plate 129
Plastic Tote Bag, Gerber Baby in Light Blue "...Over 50 Years", Early 80's $3.00
Plate 130
Plastic Tote Bag, Gerber Baby in Light Blue "...Over 60 Years", Late 80's $3.00
Plate 131
Plastic Tote Bag, Gerber Baby in Dark Blue "...Over 60 Years", Early 90's $3.00
Plate 132
Gerber Baby 12" tray, 1978.. $15.00

Photo Index and Price Guide (continued)

Plastic 134
    Gerber Baby Frisbee, "Safety Comes in Cans", 1980's $7.00
Plate 135
    Sports Pouch, 1990's $9.00
Plate 136
    Gerber Balloons, 1990's $1.00
Plate 137
    Beach Towel with "50 Years of Caring. 1978" $15.00
Plate 138
    Gerber Baby Beach Towel, 1988 . . . . $15.00
Plate 139
    Rayon Canvas Windjammer Duffel Bag, 1983 . . . . $18.00
Plate 140
    Gerber Baby Tote Bag, 1990's $15.00
Plate 141
    Plastic Stadium Cushion, 1980's $15.00
Plate 142
    Leather Golf Glove, 1980's $10.00
    Greenskeeper, 1983 . . . . $10.00
    3 Golf Balls in a Box, 1978 . . . . $10.00
    Golf Tees in Plastic Holder, Printed, 1970's $7.00
Plate 143
    Double Deck Red and Blue Playing Cards in Plastic Case, 1978 . . . . $10.00
    Double Deck Red and Blue Playing Cards in Cardboard Case, 1978 . . . . $8.00
    Double Deck Green and White Playing Cards in Cardboard Case, Modilac, 1970's $10.00
    Gerber Baby Single Deck of Playing Cards, Dark Blue $7.00
Plate 144
    Gerber Baby Single Deck of Card, Blue on White $7.00
    Double Deck Blue and White Playing Cards in Cardboard Case, Modilac, 1970's $12.00
Plate 145
    Single Deck of Cards Made for the Japaneese Market, 1970's $20.00
    Single Deck of Cards Featuring the Sun Rubber Gerber Baby Doll, 1955 . . . . $45.00
Plate 146
    Gerber Spalding Tennis Balls, 3 in Can, 1978 . . . . $10.00
Plate 147
    Single Gerber Baby Tennis Ball, 1978 . . . . $4.00
Plate 148
    Gerber White Sports Hat, 1978 . . . . $9.00
Plate 149
    Gerber Baby Running Shorts, 1978 . . . . $7.00

Time and Temperature

Plate 150
    Food Timer: Safety/ Gerber/ Takes time $10.00
Plate 151
    Gerber Baby Outdoor Thermometer, 50 Years of Caring, 1980's $15.00
Plate 152
    Travel Alarm Clock, 1990's $15.00
    Wall Clock, 1990's $20.00
    Deck Clock, 1990's $15.00
Plate 153
    Wood Framed, Hexagon Shape Wall Clock, 1970's $40.00

Photo Index and Price Guide (continued)

Toys

Plate 154
 Gerber Lacing Shoe in Original Box, 1969 . . . . $25.00
Plate 155
 Gerber Baby Swiss Bell, 1969 . . . . $35.00
Plate 156
 Gerber Baby Talk Back Phone, 1969 . . . . $35.00
Plate 157
 Gerber Jingle Blox in Original Box,1950's $45.00
Plate 158
 Gerber Baby Strained Foods Jar Squeaky Toy, Prototype $250.00
Plate 159
 Gerber Tender Loving Care Bears with Tag, 1978 . . . . $25.00
Plate 160
 Gerber Precious Plush Stuffed Rabbit, 1970's $15.00
Plate 161
 Gerber Tender Loving Care Bear without Tag, 1978 . . . . $10.00
 Gerber Baby Bib, 1990's. $1.00
Plate 162
 6" Stuffed Animals made by Atlanta Novelty, Early 80's $8.00
Plate 163
 Teddy Bear Rattle. 1970,s $20.00
Plate 164
 Carrying Case of Miniature Toy Gerber Baby Care Products, Early 1980's $20.00
Plate 165
 Gerber Baby Blankie Bear, 1990's $6.00
Plate 166
 Gerber Baby Activity Mirror, 1994 . . . . $15.00
Plate 167
 Gerber Soft Touch Story Book, 1994 . . . . $15.00
Plate 168
 Gerber The Magic Message Phone, 1994 . . . . $30.00
Plate 169
 Gerber Musical Dreamer Activity Screen, 1994 . . . . $25.00
Plate 170
 Gerber Baby Activity Computer, 1994 . . . . $30.00
Plate 171
 Gerber 1,2,3 Discover, 1994. . . . . $20.00
Plate 172
 Gerber Magic Musical Doodler, 1995 . . . . $25.00
Plate 173
 Gerber Electronic Discovery Book, 1995. . . . . $23.00

Trucks and Trains

Plate 174
 Gerber Semi Made by Winross, 9 1/2 ", 1978 . . . . $250.00
Plate 175
 Gerber GMC 18 Wheeler by Nylint, 1979 . . . . $80.00
Plate 176
 Gerber Box Car-Blue, HO Gauge, by Bachman, 1978 . . . . $95.00

Photo Index and Price Guide (continued)

Plate 177
>Gerber Box Car, Pink, by Tyco (Repro of Bachman box car) $30.00

Plate 178
>Gerber Baby Food Reefer, O Gauge by Lionel,1979 . . . . $95.00

Plate 179
>Gerber Baby Food Reefer, Large Scale by Lionel in Green, 1990 . . . . $75.00

Gerber Visitor Center, Gerber Guest House

Plate 180
>Complimentary Gift Box with Tumblers and Spoon, Early 1990's $25.00

Plate 181
>Visitor's Center Packet with 6 items, 1950's $75.00

Plate 182
>Visitor's Center Folder with Baby Picture, 3D Glasses, and Facts Folder, 1990's $15.00
>Visitor Center Yellow Cardboard Flyer, 1990 . . . . $2.00
>"Baby Takes", Card Which Explains the 3D Movie Shown a the Visitor Center, 1990's $2.00

Plate 183
>"Welcome To The Gerber House"- a 5 page History of Gerber and the Family $5.00
>Small Glass Marked "Gerber Guest House", 1990 . . . . $8.00

PLATE 184
>Styrofoam "Koozie Kup®" with "Gerber" and the Baby on One Side, 1980's $10.00

Plate 185
>Reverse Side with Lighted Bulb and "Safety/Is Just a Thought Away"

Plate 186
>"Toy" Full Size Juice Cans $8.00

Magazine Ads

>1928-1960's $5- $10.00
>1970's and 1980's $4.00
>Special Ads featuring Premium Offers or Gerber Family Children . . . . $8.00-$20.00